IMAGES
of America

OAK CREEK
WISCONSIN

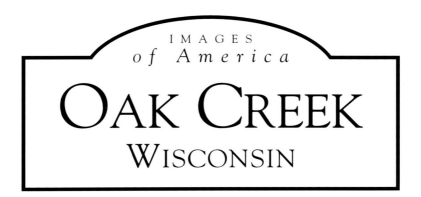

Oak Creek
Wisconsin
Images of America

Anita and Larry Rowe

Copyright © 1998 by Anita and Larry Rowe
ISBN 0-7385-4923-1

Published by Arcadia Publishing
Charleston SC, Chicago IL, Portsmouth NH, San Francisco CA

Printed in the United States of America

Library of Congress Catalog Card Number: 2006930420

For all general information contact Arcadia Publishing at:
Telephone 843-853-2070
Fax 843-853-0044
E-mail sales@arcadiapublishing.com
For customer service and orders:
Toll-Free 1-888-313-2665

Visit us on the Internet at http://www.arcadiapublishing.com

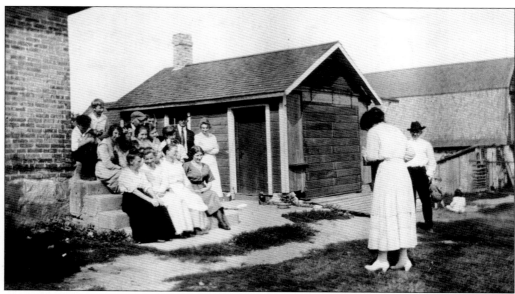

RESIDENTS POSING FOR A PHOTOGRAPH ON THE ZIMDARS FARM, ON THE SOUTHEAST CORNER OF HOWELL AND OAKWOOD ROADS. The exact date is unknown, but it is probably the late 1920s or early 1930s. The only person identified is Minnie Last Zimdars, seated in the front row wearing the white apron. (Courtesy of Carolyn Haack.)

Contents

1. Farms and Families — 7

2. Places to Go and People to See — 25

3. Where We Learned and Where We Worshipped — 41

4. Special Times and Special Places — 53

5. The Lay of the Land — 85

6. Becoming a City — 97

Acknowledgments — 128

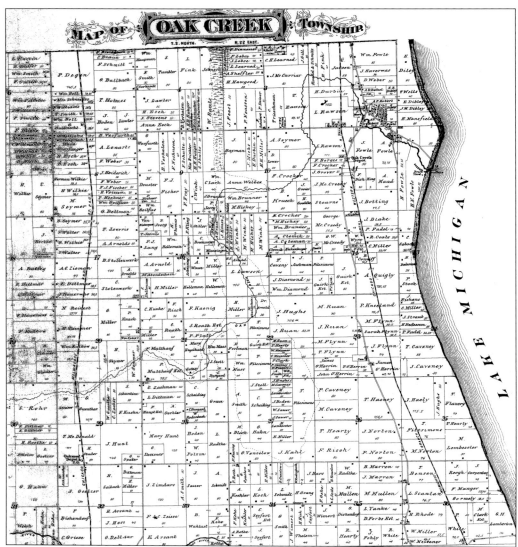

PLAT MAP SHOWING THE NAMES OF LAND OWNERS OF THE OAK CREEK AREA IN 1876. At this time Oak Creek and what was to be South Milwaukee were one township. In 1897 most of the northeast corner of this area became the city of South Milwaukee. The rest of Oak Creek remained a township until 1955. (Courtesy of Oak Creek Historical Society.)

One

FARMS AND FAMILIES

Easily one of Oak Creek's most important characteristics is the legacy that its long time residents and farmers provided. Farming was the prominent occupation well into the 1950s, and many of the town's best-known residents worked Oak Creek's soil for many years. The families that lived in the area became the town's backbone, turning hard work and traditions into the strength it would need to survive.

These farms and homesteads would give way to subdivisions, with house upon house dotting the landscape. With the change from township to city status, Oak Creek would become another one of Southeast Wisconsin's suburbs, where many of Milwaukee's residents would move to escape the problems of the big city.

However, the area's first settlers would leave behind street names and stories to pass on, and lay the foundation that would give Oak Creek its own special look. And with this look back we can see how much has changed, while still admiring the people that decided Oak Creek would be the place where they would spend their lives.

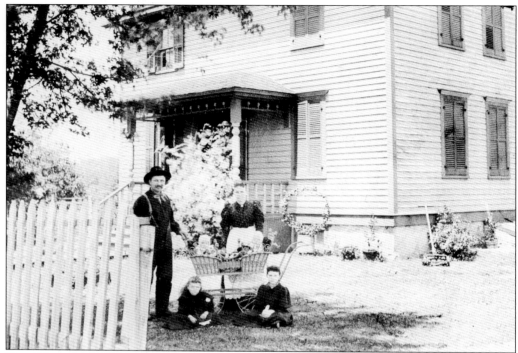

THE WOHLUST FAMILY ON THEIR HOMESTEAD, 1700 OAKWOOD ROAD. Taken in 1896, Ernst Wohlust is shown with his wife, Anna, six-month-old twins Edgar and Edna (in the carriage), and daughters Ida (left) and Louise. Ernst was a blacksmith by trade, and Edgar would eventually follow in his father's occupation. (Courtesy of CNI Newspapers.)

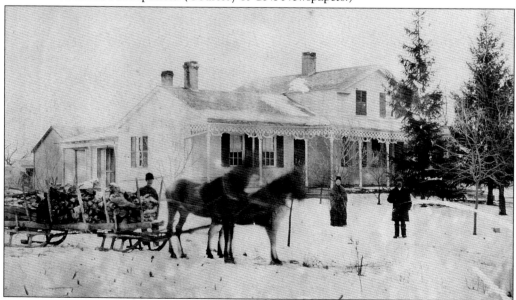

THE HONADEL HOME ON THE CORNER OF WHAT IS NOW SOUTH 27TH STREET AND PUETZ ROAD, ABOUT 1875. The horse-drawn sleigh is carrying firewood to heat the home and feed the wood-burning stove. (Courtesy of Elroy and Nancy Honadel.)

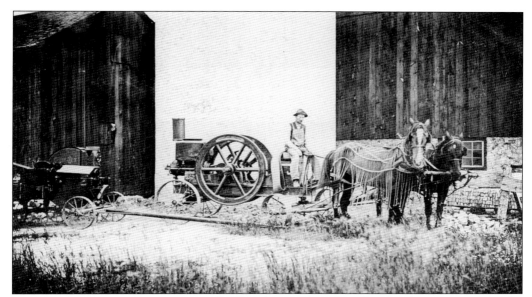

FRED LUENEBERG JR., POSING WITH HIS NEW BELLE CITY SILO FILLER, AROUND 1918. Belle City farm equipment was made in Racine, Wisconsin, and this particular implement could also be used to grind feed. Note the fringes on the horses that were known as "Fly Chasers." These would keep flies from pestering the horse by the motion of the fringes while the animal moved. The photograph was taken on the Lueneberg farm at 128 East Ryan Road. (Courtesy of CNI Newspapers.)

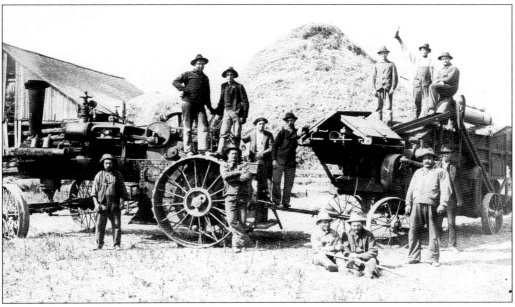

LOCAL FARMERS THRESHING ON A FARM NEAR ELM AND NICHOLSON, C. 1910. The men pictured are, from left to right: (standing) Karl Schelke, Emil Schumacher, Arthur Rothe, Ferdinand Rothe, Dan Goelzer, Edward Studer, Albert Studer, Louis Hess, Herman Schumacher, Ernest Schumacher, and Louis Goelzer; (seated) a man remembered as "Little John" and August Teargarden. (Courtesy of CNI Newspapers.)

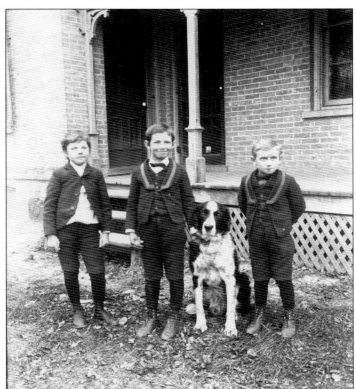

ART, CHARLES, AND LEON ZIMDARS, POSING WITH THE FAMILY DOG ON THE ZIMDARS FARM, C. 1905. The farm was located on the southeast corner of Howell and Oakwood Roads. (Courtesy of Carolyn Haack.)

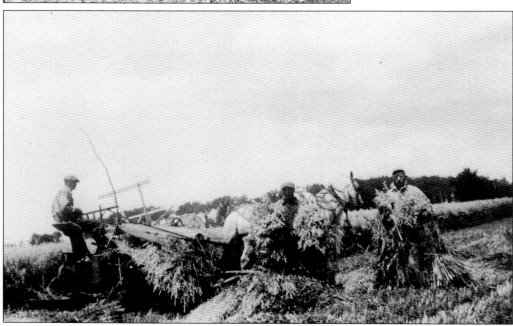

CUTTING OATS ON THE HEYMANN FARM, LOCATED ON THE 7300 BLOCK OF HOWELL AVENUE. The photo was taken on July 29, 1936. This farm was located in the area north of where the Oak Creek water tower now stands. (Courtesy of Eleanore and Alfred Hauerwas.)

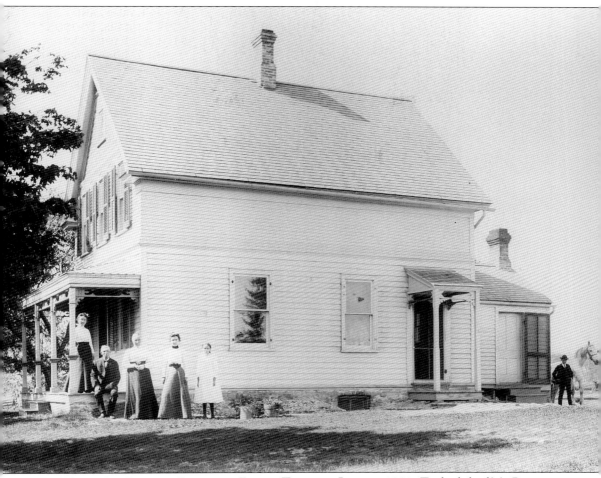

THE FAMILY OF PATRICK RYAN IN A PHOTO TAKEN IN JULY OF 1901. To the left of Mr. Ryan is his daughter Nora, and on the right is his wife, Mary, his daughter Mary, and Margaret Goumper. Margaret was an orphan that the Ryans raised. The man at the rear of the house is unidentified. Presumably, Ryan Road was named after Patrick Ryan, and by some accounts Ryan Road was the first paved road in Wisconsin. The house was located at South Chicago and Ryan Roads. Nora Ryan was a teacher at Scanlan School from 1914 to 1934. (Courtesy of Oak Creek Historical Society.)

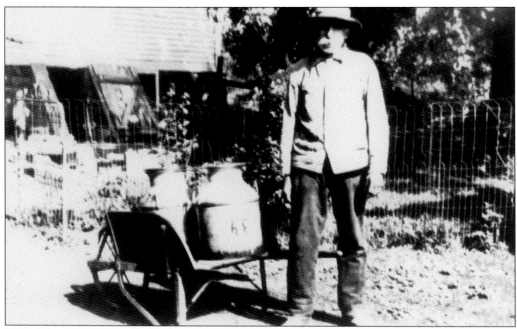

FRED MEYER, ON THE MEYER FARM, LOCATED ON 27TH STREET AND RYAN ROAD, 1920s. Fred is carting back empty milk cans that the Gridley Dairy in Milwaukee returned and left on the street in front of the house. Note the number "39" on the can. Each farm had their own number on their milk cans to identify where they came from. (Courtesy of LeRoy and Beulah Meyer.)

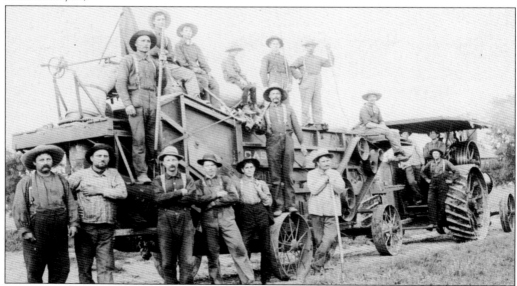

THE GUSTAVE ARSAND FARM, LOCATED AT HOWELL AND OAKWOOD, IN THE EARLY 1900s. From left to right are: (foreground) Gustave Arsand, August Wrasse, Ed Arsand, Henry Zeisse, John Zeisse, Frank Dallman (on wheel), and William Last; (on threshing rig) John Zimdars, William Scheiding, Roy Arsand, George Arsand, Leo Zimdars, Bill Block, Charles Roth, and Joe Joerres. The man at the extreme left was not identified. (Courtesy of CNI Newspapers.)

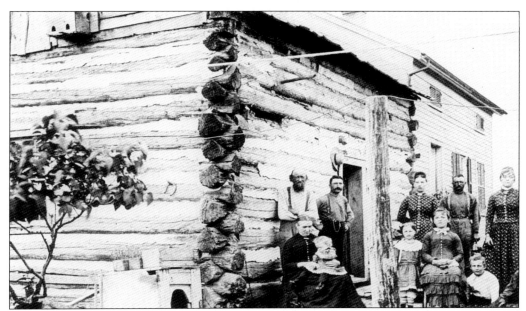

THE JOHN AND MARY BERTKE FARM, C. 1880S. The log cabin portion, built in 1839, was used as the summer kitchen at the time of this photo. The farm was located at what is now 8047 South 13th Street. Mary Bertke is seated with child. The man with the beard is John's brother William, who owned a farm in Franklin, Wisconsin. The man with his hands on his hips is believed to be John Bertke. (Courtesy of Andrew Janiga.)

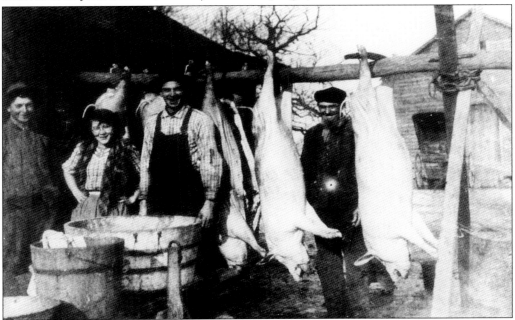

BUTCHERING HOGS AT THE CHRIS SCHERBARTH FARM IN OAK CREEK. Butchering your own livestock was a common practice on farms. It was usually done in the fall of the year. The device used to hang the hogs by their legs was called a gambrel stick. (Courtesy of LeRoy and Beulah Meyer.)

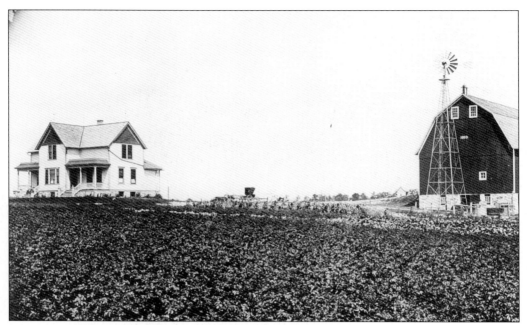

THE MAHR FARM, LOCATED AT 10820 27TH STREET. The house was built in 1908 at a cost of a little over $2,000. In later years, the Mahrs would have one of three major apple orchards in the area. (Courtesy of Violet Mahr.)

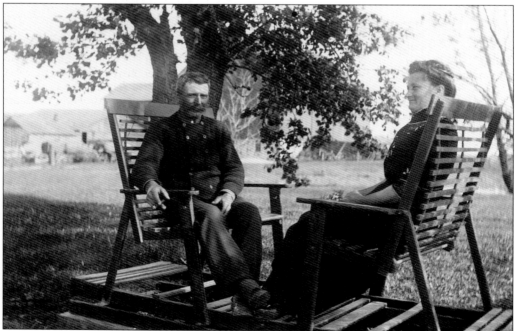

MR. AND MRS. HERMAN FRANKE, RELAXING ON THEIR FARM, LOCATED ON 27TH STREET AND DREXEL AVENUE. The summer kitchen from this farm was donated to the Oak Creek Historical Society and is now part of the museum complex located at 15th and Forest Hill Avenue. (Courtesy of Oak Creek Historical Society.)

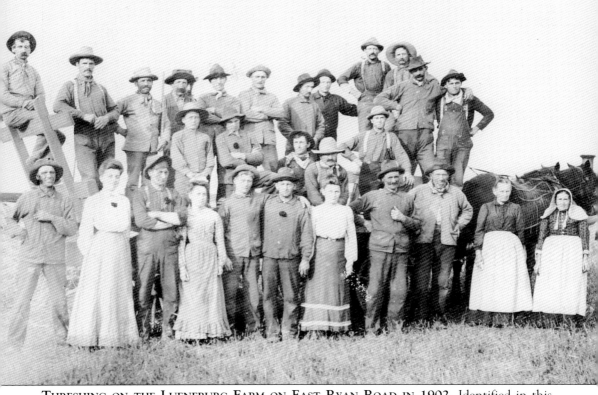

THRESHING ON THE LUENEBURG FARM ON EAST RYAN ROAD IN 1902. Identified in this picture are, from left to right: (lower) William Joerres, Helen Mauer, Fred Lueneburg Jr., Mary Martin, William Blomberg, Frank Martson, Helen Lueneburg, Fred Lueneburg Sr., Carl Tietz, Mrs. Fred Lueneburg, and Mrs. Lueneburg (grandmother); (center) Albert Blomberg, William Lueneburg, Art Schmidt, Christ Brinkman, and Harry Hahn; (top) George Manka, Alex Popa, John Dill, Carl Polits, William Brinkman (behind Polits), Gust Martson, Fred Roth, Henry Seymer, William Seymer, August Blomberg, Albert Dittmar, William Lueneburg, and Philip Roth. (Courtesy of CNI Newspapers.)

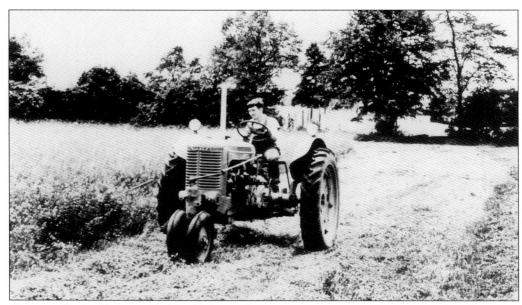

GORDON ESCH, RIDING A NEW JI CASE TRACTOR ON THE FAMILY FARM. This photo was taken in 1941. The farm was located along 13th Avenue, between Drexel and Rawson Avenues, and ran west to what is now Interstate 94. (Courtesy of Gordon and Dolores Esch.)

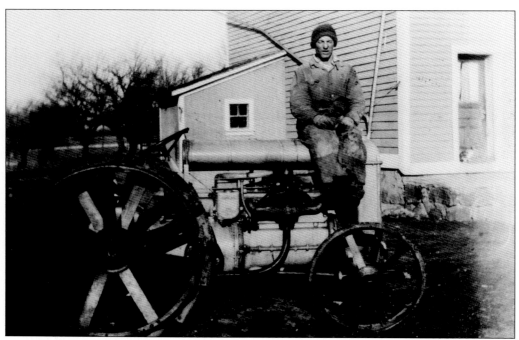

JOHN HEYMANN, PAUSING FOR A PICTURE ON HIS TRACTOR. The farm was then located around the 7300 block of Howell Avenue and was approximately 25 acres. The photo was taken around the 1930s. (Courtesy of Eleanore and Alfred Hauerwas.)

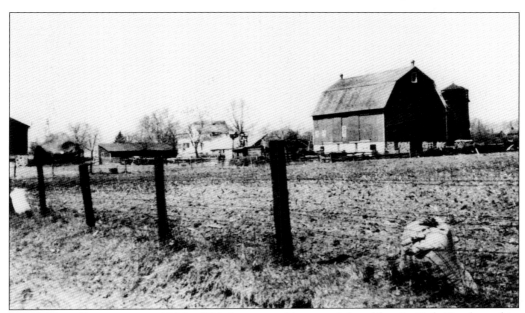

THE MEYER FARM IN THE 1930S. This homestead is one of the oldest in Oak Creek, and in 1998 LeRoy and Beulah Meyer were awarded a special Sesquicentennial homestead certificate to coincide with Wisconsin's 150th year of statehood. The Meyers were also known for their apple orchard. (Courtesy of LeRoy and Beulah Meyer.)

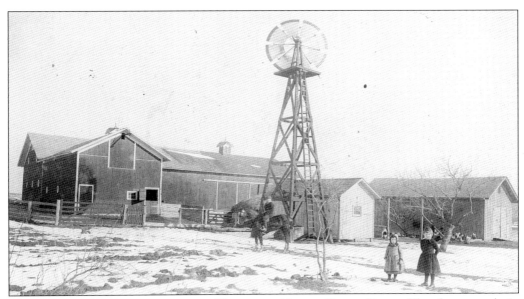

THE HONADEL FARM, LOCATED ON HIGHWAY 41 AND PUETZ ROAD. The three people in the picture were visiting relatives—Louis, Ada, and Mae Brunn. (Courtesy of Elroy and Nancy Honadel.)

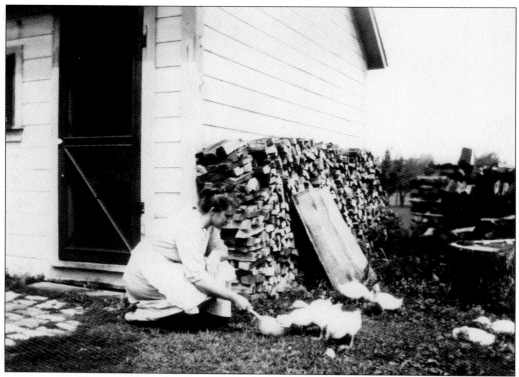

BERTHA MAASS (NEE KEHE), FEEDING POULTRY ON THE MAASS FARM. The farm was located on the east side of Nicholson Road, north of Ryan Road. This picture was taken around the 1920s. (Courtesy of Oak Creek Historical Society.)

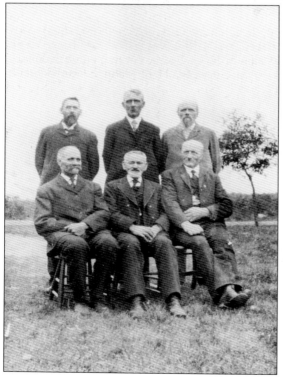

GROUP PHOTO, PROBABLY TAKEN ON THE SEYMER FARM ON THE SOUTHEAST CORNER OF NICHOLSON ROAD AND DREXEL AVENUE, BEFORE 1907. Seated from left to right are John Tabor Feldkamp, Anton F.T. Seymer, and August Seymer. Standing from left to right are Albert Dresselhouse, Henry Kothe, and Barney Bertke. (Courtesy of Andrew Janiga.)

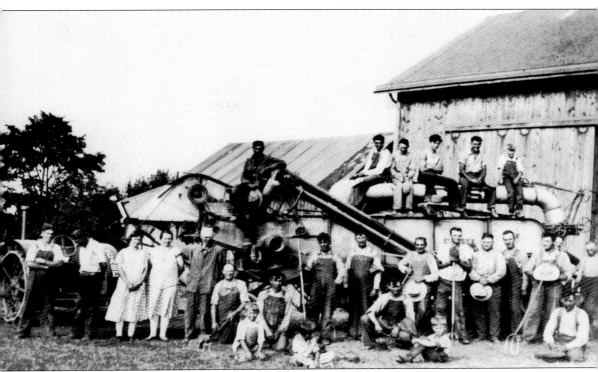

THRESHING PHOTO TAKEN ON AN OAK CREEK FARM ON SEPTEMBER 18, 1927. Taking part in the operation that day were, from left to right: (on top of the rig) Fred Lueneburg Jr., Walter Schmidt, Lester Phohl, William Peters, Fred Schultz, and Loren Lueneburg; (standing) Alvin Guckenberger, Klemence Lueneburg, Frieda Utech, Mrs. Edward Schmidt, Fred Lueneburg Sr., Peter Mueller, Martin Verdev, Emil Klemky, Ralph Spencer, George Arsand, Frank Sedmineg, Hubert Joerres, John Wrasse, and Charles Bosse; (kneeling men) Harry Hahn, Edward Schmidt, Adolph Schmidt, and William Schmidt; (the three boys) Howard Schmidt, Arvin Hahn, and Harry Schmidt. (Courtesy of CNI Newspapers.)

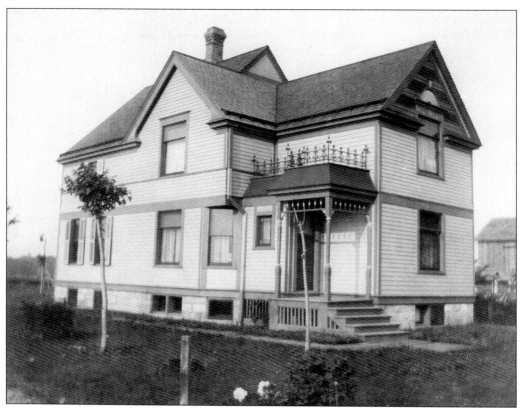

THE GUSTAVE MILLER FARM, LOCATED ON THE SOUTHWEST CORNER OF HOWELL AND PUETZ. The shed from this farm was later donated to the Oak Creek Historical Society complex. (Courtesy of Oak Creek Historical Society.)

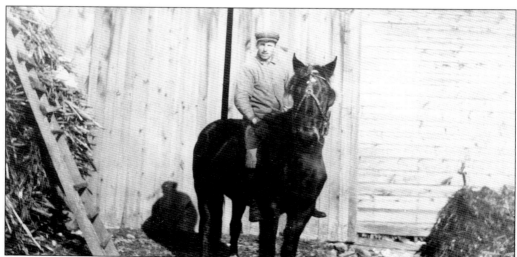

WILLIAM SCHEIDING, TAKEN ABOUT THE TIME OF WORLD WAR I ON THE HENRY SCHEIDING FARM. William was a farmer, hunter, and carpenter. This photo was taken and developed by Leon B. Zimdars. (Courtesy of Oak Creek Historical Society.)

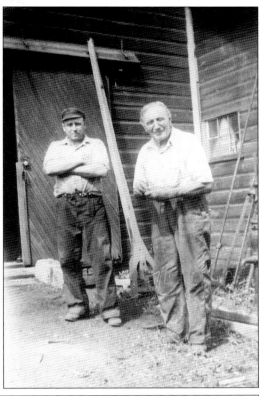

EDGAR (ON THE LEFT) AND HIS FATHER, ERNST WOHLUST, AT THEIR BLACKSMITH SHOP ON NICHOLSON AND OAKWOOD ROAD IN 1937. The shop and its contents were moved to the Oak Creek Historical Society Museum Complex in 1968. Of the eight Oak Creek-area blacksmith shops, this was the only one that was rescued. (Courtesy of Oak Creek Historical Society.)

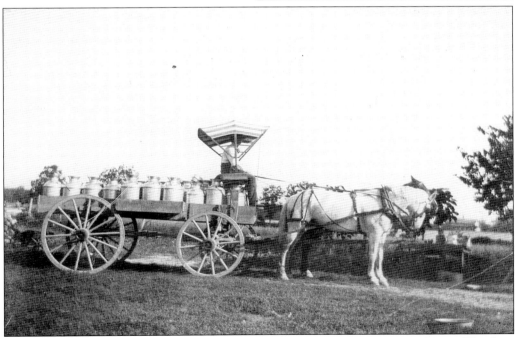

HAULING MILK TO TOWN BY HORSE-DRAWN WAGON FROM THE HONADEL FARM. The farm was located on 27th Street and Puetz Road. (Courtesy of Elroy and Nancy Honadel.)

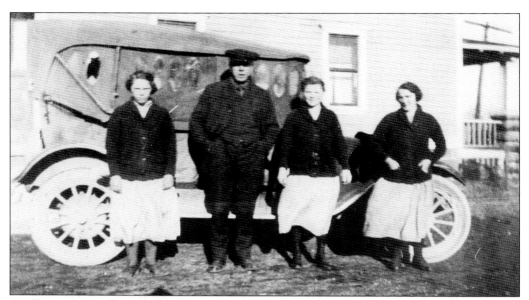

AN EARLY 1920S PHOTO TAKEN IN THE 7300 BLOCK OF SOUTH HOWELL AVENUE. From left to right are: Clara Hauerwas, her husband, Frank Hauerwas, and Clara's sisters, Dorothy and Kathleen Heymann. The car they are standing in front of is Frank's 1917 Dodge. (Courtesy of Eleanore and Alfred Hauerwas.)

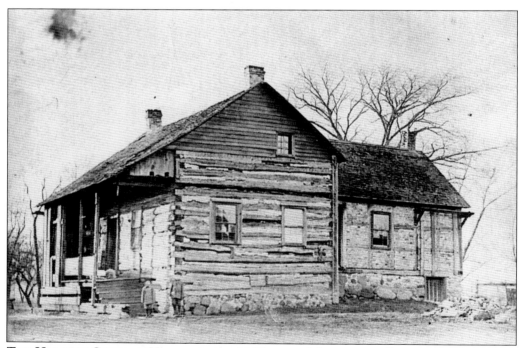

THE HOME OF GUSTAVE VANSELOW, IN 1917, WITH MARLIN AND SYLVESTER VANSELOW. This cabin was also the home of Gustave's parents, Gottlieb and Wilhelmina Vanselow. It was located just west of Oakwood Road. (Courtesy of Neal Raduenz.)

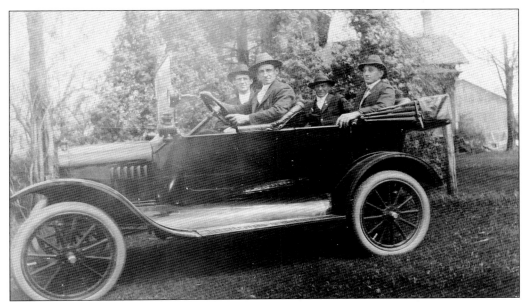

LEON AND CHARLES ZIMDARS, WITH TWO OF THEIR COUSINS, ON THE ZIMDARS'S FARM, c. 1930. (Courtesy of Carolyn Haack.)

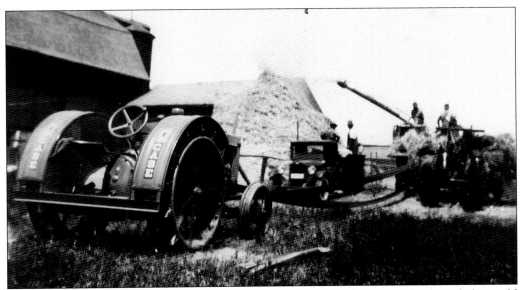

AN EARLY 1930s PHOTO OF THRESHING ON THE HONADEL FARM. The long belt would provide the power from the tractor to run the threshing machine. (Courtesy of Elroy and Nancy Honadel.)

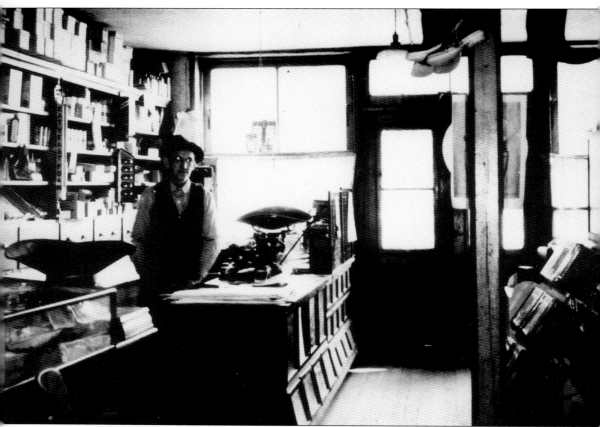

LOUIS H. GOELZER, STANDING IN HIS GENERAL STORE IN 1912. The store was located in the basement of Studer's Oakwood Hall, later known as the Cellar Restaurant. The area of Oak Creek that was known as the town of Oakwood was located in the general area of what is now Oakwood Road, between South 13th Street and South Howell Avenue. (Courtesy of LeRoy and Beulah Meyer.)

Two

PLACES TO GO AND PEOPLE TO SEE

Several smaller towns made up the area that was known as the Township of Oak Creek. Names like Klondike, Oakwood, Otjen, and Carrollville are still used to describe distinctive areas in Oak Creek. Within these towns, there would of course be a need for supplies, services, and diversions to make life a little easier in the midst of all that hard work. The larger companies would build in the Carrollville area, in the township's southeast corner. Smaller businesses would spring up all over the area to meet the needs of Oak Creek's growing population. Very few of the buildings that were homes to these early businessmen and women remain, but their goods and services became another sizable part of the area's history. Local government would also provide needed services to its citizens. The town would also find out the hard way that sometimes essential services were lacking. But these were a part of the growing pains of progress—the same progress that would again bring a new look to the area. Looking at these scenes, you can almost hear the music and conversations that would be an everyday part of their lives. And certainly, the memories of the trips to these special places would last a lifetime.

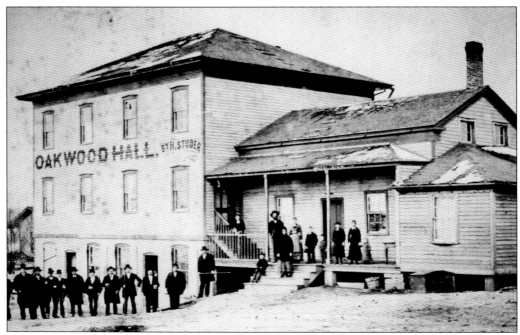

HENRY STUDERS'S OAKWOOD HALL. Built in the 1870s, Henry Studers's Oakwood Hall would, over the years, house a general store, a saloon, living quarters for the Studer family, rooms for boarders, a dance hall on the third floor, and a restaurant. (Courtesy of LeRoy and Beulah Meyer.)

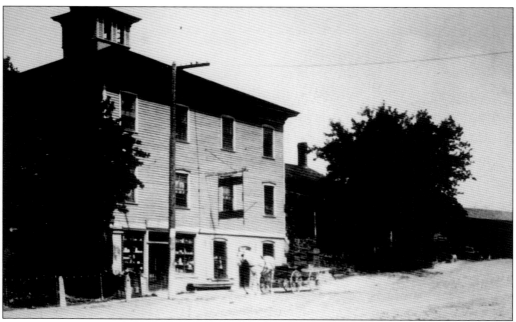

ANOTHER VIEW OF STUDERS'S, EARLY 1900S. This view shows the entrance to the general store. (Courtesy of LeRoy and Beulah Meyer.)

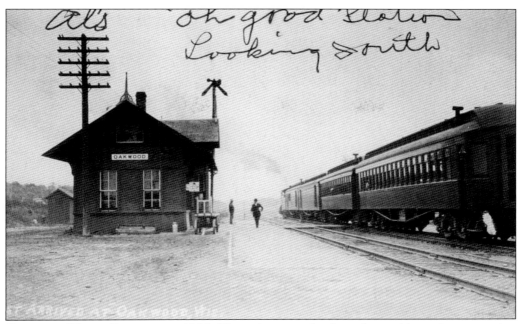

OAKWOOD TRAIN STATION, C. 1910. The train stopped twice a day at this station, one going to, and one coming from, Milwaukee. (Courtesy of LeRoy and Beulah Meyer.)

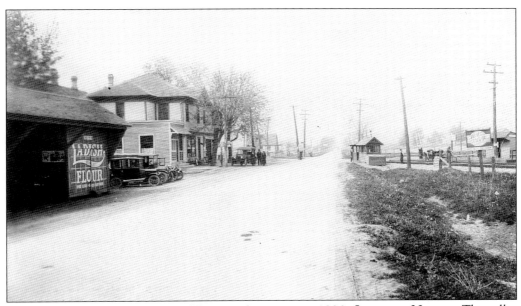

THE CORNER OF RAWSON AND HOWELL AVENUE, IN 1930, LOOKING NORTH. The taller building in this photo is the Green Frog Inn. The smaller building to the south housed a blacksmith shop and garage, which later burned in July of 1930. (Courtesy of Oak Creek Historical Society.)

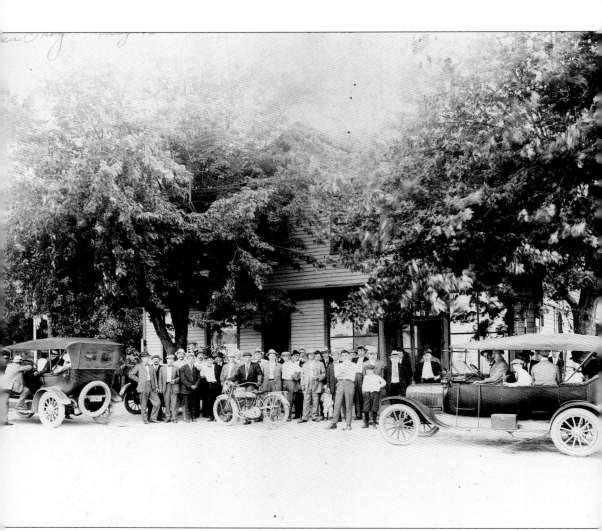

ANOTHER SCENE FROM THE GREEN FROG INN IN THE 1930S. On January 1, 1935, the Green Frog Inn, which at that time was known as the Dells, burned. There were only a few New Year's visitors in the place at the time it caught fire, and all were able to escape unharmed. The heat from the blaze was so intense that traffic on both Howell and Rawson Avenues was stopped, along with the North Shore Electric Line Cars. Since neighboring fire departments refused to respond to the fire at the Dells, its demise was the catalyst for Oak Creek to form its own fire department. (Courtesy of Oak Creek Historical Society.)

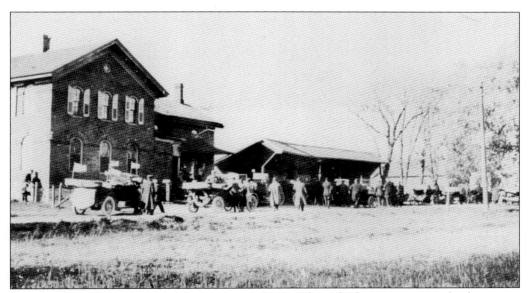

THE JOERRES TAVERN, AS IT APPEARED IN 1918. Through the years it was also known as Munzinger's and Breezy's. The building was located at 8011 South Howell Avenue and was razed to make room for the A.C. Spark Plug Plant. (Courtesy of CNI Newspapers.)

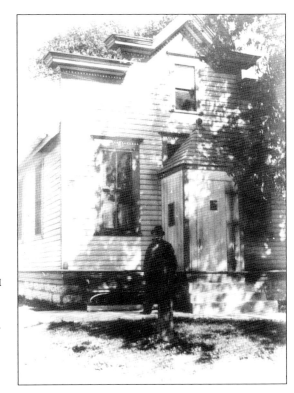

THE WILLMS TAVERN, LOCATED NORTH OF RAWSON AVENUE ON 13TH STREET. The man in the picture is John Willms. This picture was taken in the early 1930s. The building was demolished in 1963 to make way for the approach of the Interstate 94 interchange. (Courtesy of Oak Creek Historical Society.)

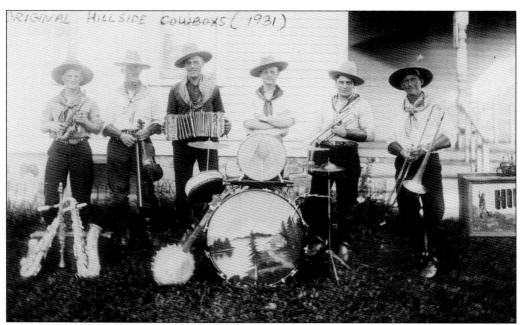

THE ORIGINAL HILLSIDE COWBOYS, 1931. They were one of the most popular bands in the Oak Creek area at that time. The band included a number of prominent Oak Creek citizens, including Art Abendschein, Fred Brinkman, and Edgar Wohlust. (Courtesy of Oak Creek Historical Society.)

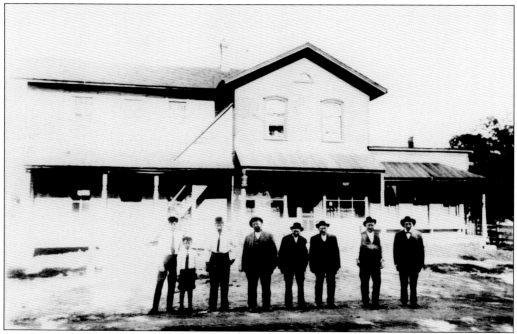

YACKY'S TAVERN IN THE LATE 1800S. It is now known as Ray Bussler's Restaurant. The building is on what was known at that time as Kilbourn Road, now South 27th Street in Oak Creek's southwest corner. (Courtesy of LeRoy and Beulah Meyer.)

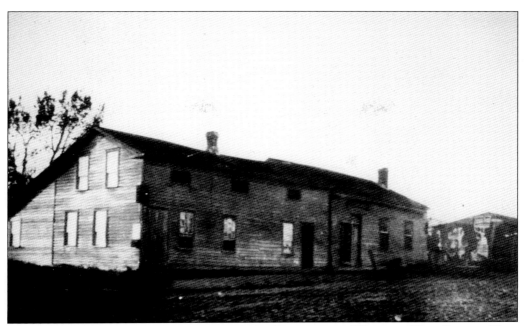

The Old Buckhorn Tavern in the 1880s, Located at What is Now South 27th Street and Ryan Road. In the early days of the Buckhorn, it served as a stage coach stop. It also served as a post office for the town of Painsville, and a stop for farmers hauling hay to Milwaukee. (Courtesy of LeRoy and Beulah Meyer.)

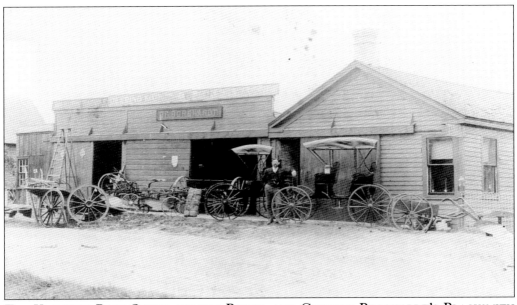

The Klondike Post Office, on the Right, and Gustave Borchardt's Blacksmith Shop, Near the Corner of New Road (Now South 13th Street) and Drexel Avenue, Early 1900s. The post office was originally the Bertke School, built in 1842. It was purchased by Gustave Borchardt in 1897 for $19 and then moved to this spot. (Courtesy of Karen Borchardt.)

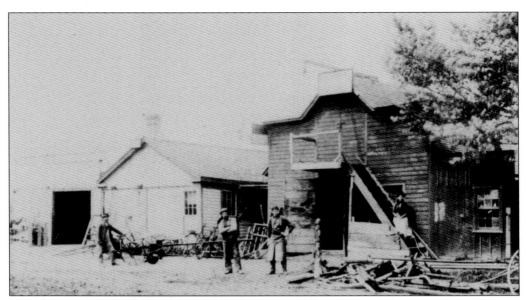

THE SCHERBARTH'S BLACKSMITH SHOP, LOCATED NEXT TO THE KLONDIKE POST OFFICE, ON THE CORNER OF SOUTH 13TH STREET AND DREXEL AVENUE. Shown in the photo are, from left to right: Gustave Borchardt (Henry Scherbarth's helper), Henry Scherbarth, and Elsie Borchardt. Elsie Borchardt later married Henry's brother Carl. Carl Scherbarth worked with his brother at this blacksmith shop in 1901. (Courtesy of LeRoy and Beulah Meyer.)

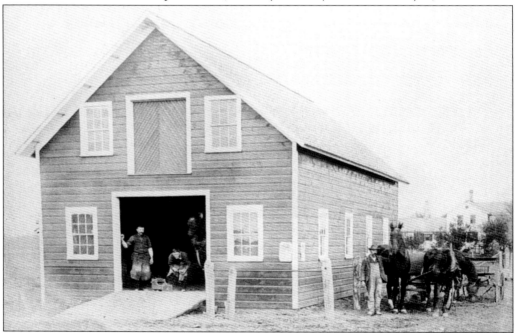

THE WOHLUST BLACKSMITH SHOP ON OAKWOOD AND NICHOLSON ROADS, 1897. Identified from left to right are: Ernst Wohlust, his assistant, Ed Prohl, and the man by the wagon is unknown. At the extreme right, in the background, is Ernst's wife, Anna, and their twin children, Edgar and Edna. (Courtesy of Neal Raduenz.)

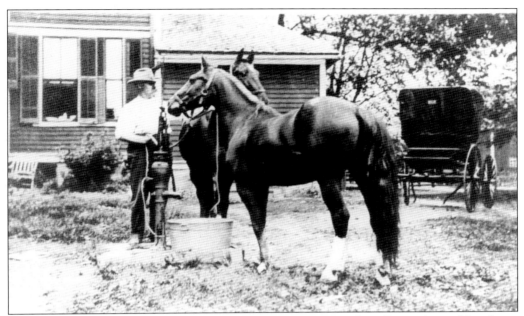

CHARLES KOEHNE, A VETERINARIAN AND BLACKSMITH IN THE OAK CREEK AREA. The photo, c. 1895, was probably taken on Koehne's property on the southwest corner of South 27th Street and Ryan Road. (Courtesy of LeRoy and Beulah Meyer.)

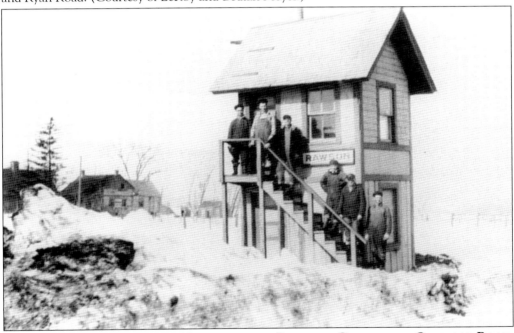

RAWSON STATION AT CHICAGO NORTHWESTERN RAILROAD CROSSING ON OAKWOOD ROAD, LOOKING NORTHWEST, IN THE LATE 1920s. Pictured from the top are: George Schwabe, Richard Vanselow, Roman Vanselow, Edward Schwabe, William Raduenz, and Gustave Vanselow. In the background to the left is the Vanselow cabin mentioned in the previous chapter. (Courtesy of Neal Raduenz.)

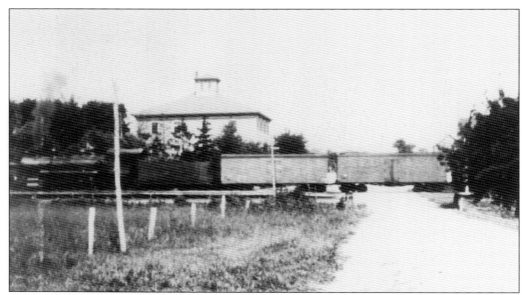

A Train, Passing Through the Oakwood Area Around 1900. In later years the tracks would be moved to the other side of town. The building behind the train is Studer's. (Courtesy of LeRoy and Beulah Meyer.)

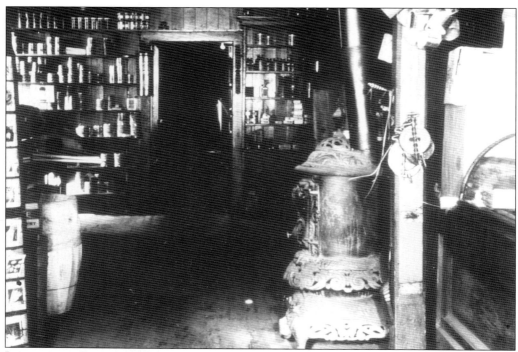

Interior of Oakwood General Store, 1912. The store was run by Louis Goelzer, and was located in the basement of Studer's on Oakwood Road. (Courtesy of LeRoy and Beulah Meyer.)

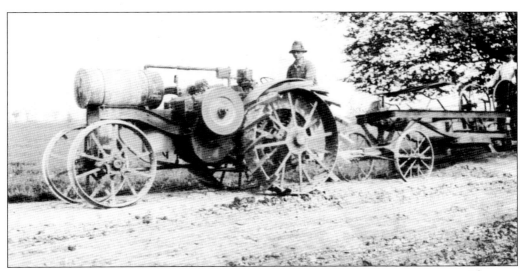

LEO ZIMDARS, PERFORMING HIS SERVICE AS A "ROADMASTER" IN APRIL OF 1911. The man in the back is unidentified. Roadmasters were appointed by the county to perform work on assigned sections of trunk roads. Zimdars was scraping a part of Howell Avenue when this photo was taken. (Courtesy of CNI Newspapers.)

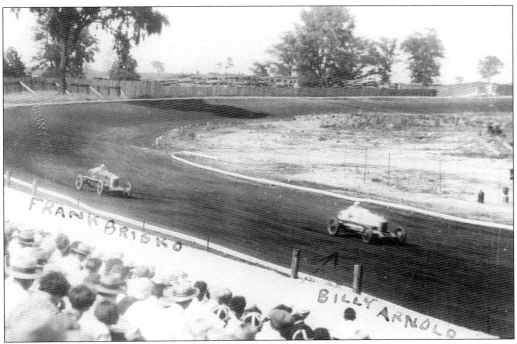

BILLY ARNOLD, WINNING A 5 KILOMETER MATCH RACE AT SOUTH MILWAUKEE SPEEDWAY ON JUNE 27, 1930. Arnold also won the Indianapolis 500 that year. His qualifying speed at Indy was 113.268 miles per hour, and his prize money was $36,800. (Courtesy of Oak Creek Historical Society.)

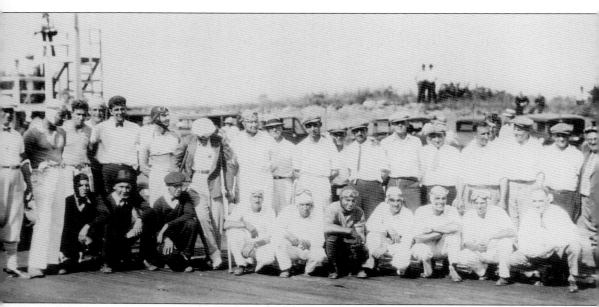

THE SOUTH MILWAUKEE SPEEDWAY ON JUNE 27, 1930. The track was located in the Carrollville area on the shores of Lake Michigan and was only in operation for a few years. The race on this day was 100 kilometers in length. The only people that were identified were, from left to right: (standing) 1-Chester Ricker, 5-George Young, 7-Chet Gardner, and 15-Grover Horn; (kneeling) 4-Wilbur Shaw, 5-Shorty Cantlon, 7-Bill Cummings, and 9-Frank Brisko. (Courtesy of Oak Creek Historical Society.)

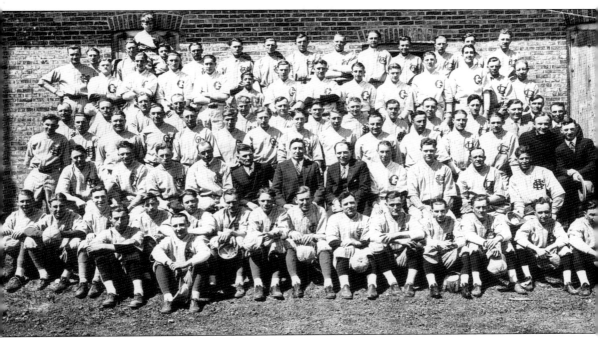

A 1927 GROUP PHOTO OF OAK CREEK AND FRANKLIN BASEBALL LEAGUE. The picture was probably taken in front of the Green Lawn School on Howell Avenue. Insignias of the teams include Green Lawn, Carrollville, Oakwood Graded, Oakwood Road, Hillside, Hickory Grove, and Kilbourn. A total of $900 was spent to uniform the entire league, which was raised by social affairs and by the passing of the hat at the games. (Courtesy of Oak Creek Historical Society.)

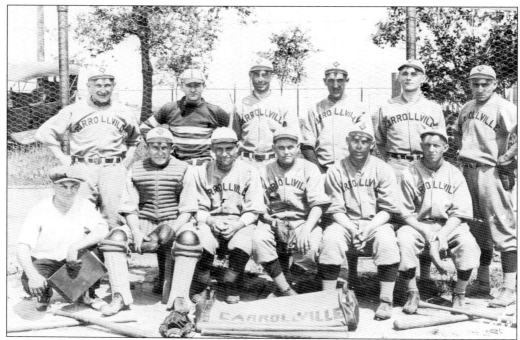

CARROLLVILLE BASEBALL TEAM, 1923. Pictured from left to right are: (seated) Joe Maresch, C. Kysely, Pete Loebel, J. Weiss, E. Duggan, and H. Schwan; (standing) Frank Kysely, Charlie Horvath, Matt Duggan, Clarence Dallmann, Elmer Loebel, and B. Grettinger. Note that the visors on most of the players had cut-outs for sunshades to allow the player to look up towards the sun at the ball. (Courtesy of CNI Newspapers.)

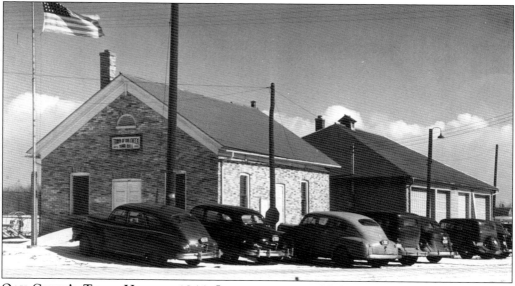

OAK CREEK'S TOWN HALL IN 1944, LOCATED ON THE NORTHEAST CORNER OF HOWELL AND PUETZ. The building to the rear was used by the Highway Department to store their large trucks. It was the first building to be moved to the corner of 15th and Forest Hill Avenue to establish the Oak Creek Historical Society. (Courtesy of Oak Creek Historical Society.)

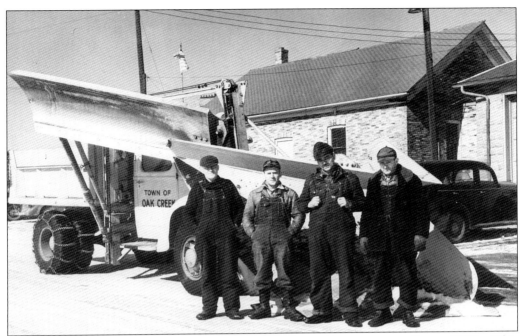

TOWN OF OAK CREEK ROAD CREW, READY TO PLOW SNOW IN THE LATE 1930S. This photo was taken next to the town hall along the Puetz Avenue side. (Courtesy of Oak Creek Historical Society.)

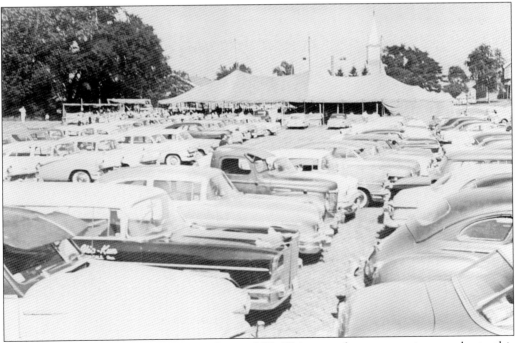

ST. MATTHEW'S CHURCH FESTIVAL, JULY 1957. This annual event remains popular to this day. St. Matthew's Church is located on South Chicago Road. (Courtesy of CNI Newspapers.)

Class of 1901.

EMMA A. MILLER,	JOSEPHINE MEYER,
ELENA B. HAHN,	MATILDA A. MORLEY.

Class of 1902.

LEO GOETSCH,	DELIA HALTER,
EDWARD BARG,	ELVIRA MAHR,
ELLA MEYER,	ELMER SCHWARTZ,
MATTIE STUDER,	HUGO ZIMMER,
JOHN SANDER,	KATIE FRANCKE.

The Graduating Class of the Oakwood High School requests your presence at the Commencement Exercises, at Molkentein's Hall, June fifteenth, nineteen hundred and one, five o'clock p. m.

COMMENCEMENT ANNOUNCEMENT FOR OAKWOOD HIGH SCHOOL, 1901. It was one of the first high schools established in the state of Wisconsin, with classes starting in 1888. Many of the children and grandchildren of these students are found living in the Oak Creek area today.

Three

WHERE WE LEARNED AND WHERE WE WORSHIPPED

Schools and churches were the lifeblood of any town that was to survive and prosper in the early days. The first settlers in Oak Creek were aware of this and established both early on. Records show that schools and churches were started in the township in the 1840s. Two of the earliest schools were Rawson School and Bertke School, both named for the men who donated the land for the schools. The denomination of the early churches would reflect the ethnic background of the immigrants that established them. St. Matthew's Catholic Church, with its first log church being built in 1841, was formed by Irish settlers. Not far behind, with its log church, would be St. John's Lutheran, built in 1843 by German immigrants. An increase in the population would spell the demise of the early schools, where all but a few of even the more modern versions of their buildings would eventually disappear. The churches, however, would change with the times, build bigger and more modern houses of worship, usually at the original location, and survive. It's a credit to any community that can keep generation after generation of families in its fold. If the churches and schools are any indication, Oak Creek has much to be proud of in this respect.

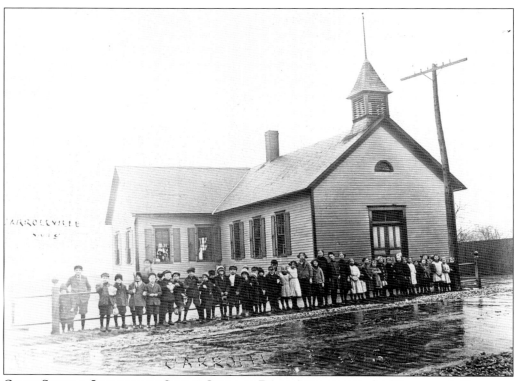

OTJEN SCHOOL, LOCATED ON SOUTH CHICAGO ROAD ACROSS FROM ST. MATTHEW'S CHURCH. The photo was taken in the early 1900s. (Courtesy of Oak Creek Historical Society.)

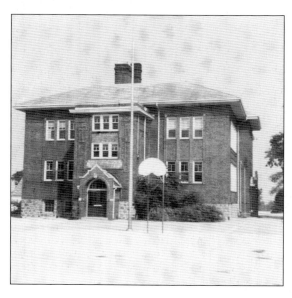

THE LAST OTJEN SCHOOL BUILDING. The school closed its doors for the final time in 1969. (Courtesy of Oak Creek Historical Society.)

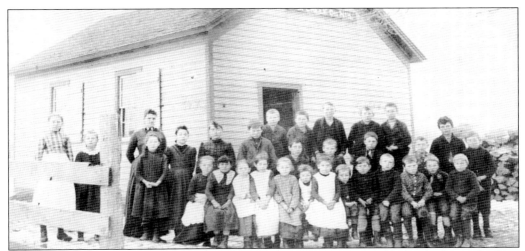

THE SCANLAN SCHOOL, C. 1890. This was the second Scanlan School, which was built in 1890 and used until 1934. A third Scanlan School was built at 10507 South Chicago Road, just south of where this building stood, closing its doors to pupils in 1976. (Courtesy of CNI Newspapers.)

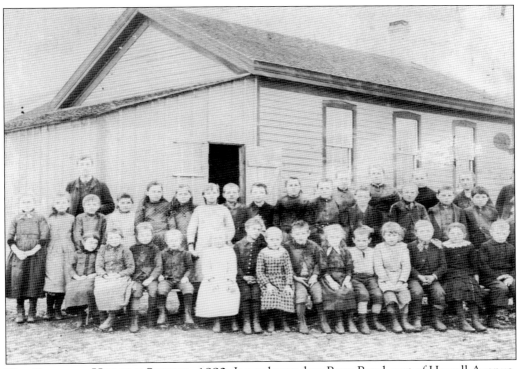

THE ORIGINAL HILLSIDE SCHOOL, 1893. It was located on Ryan Road, east of Howell Avenue. Built in 1860, the building would be sold in an auction for $11 and moved to the Seymer Farm on Howell Avenue and used as a granary. (Courtesy of CNI Newspapers.)

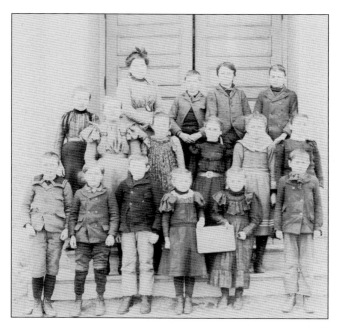

HILLSIDE SCHOOL, 1901. Shown here, from left to right, are: (front row) Charles Maass, George Roth, Arnold Tietz, Anna Schmidt, Laura Miller, and Edward Schmidt; (middle row) Anna Marcion, Emma Keske, Elsie Tietz, Agatha Roth, Helen Lueneburg, and Rosie Schmidt; (back row) teacher Berdie Kissinger, Robert Hahn, Oscar Keske, and William Lueneburg. (Courtesy of CNI Newspapers.)

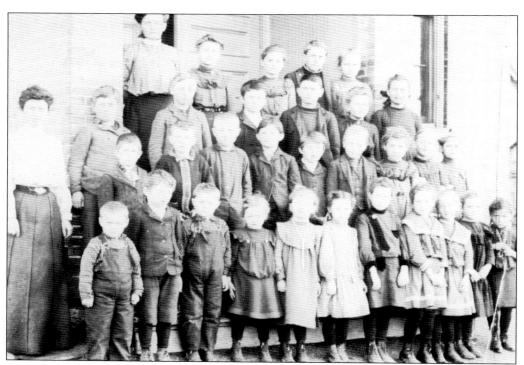

ANOTHER CLASS PHOTO OF HILLSIDE SCHOOL, 1906. The teacher (left) in this photo is Ella Zimmer. In 1934 this building was moved across the street on Ryan Road and became the shell for an expanded Hillside School. That building would hold classes until 1956, when it became the new city hall, and still later a photography studio. (Courtesy of CNI Newspapers.)

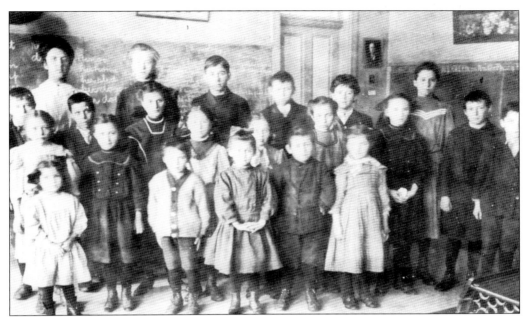

THE DISTRICT FOUR, LATER KNOWN AS HICKORY GROVE SCHOOL, 1910. Pictured from left to right are: (front row) Ester Manske, Erna Bindels, Art Manske, Lillian Hauerwas, Richard Esch, Irene Kent, and Otto Manske; (middle row) Minnie Gutknecht, Erv Manske, Charles Hauerwas, Elizabeth Willms, Edith Wilke, Frieda Kent, Lydia Schultz, Ellen Bindels, and Roman Esch; (back row) teacher Ella Quentin, Clara Prochnow, John Hauerwas, Arthur Esch, Milton Newton, and Cora Borchardt. (Courtesy of CNI Newspapers.)

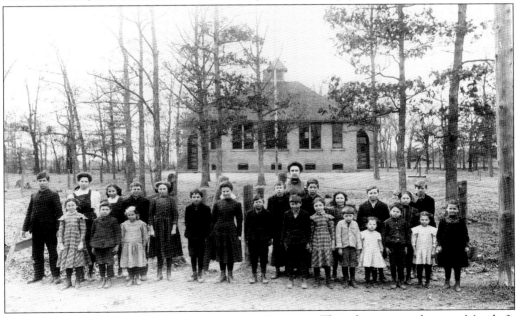

OUTSIDE CLASS PHOTO AT HICKORY GROVE SCHOOL. This photo was taken on March 3, 1911, again with Ella Quentin as teacher. Hickory Grove was located on South 13th Street, north of Drexel Avenue. (Courtesy of Oak Creek Historical Society.)

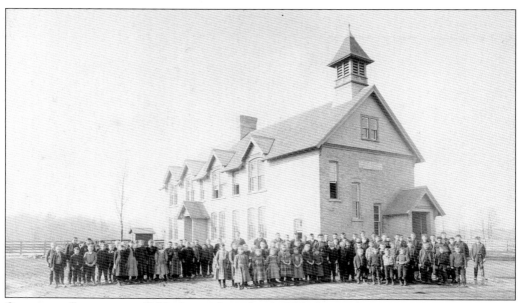

OAKWOOD SCHOOL, C. 1900. Located on South 27th Street, between Oakwood and Ryan Roads, it was part of a joint district with the town of Franklin. The building is now being used as a day care center. (Courtesy of Oak Creek Historical Society.)

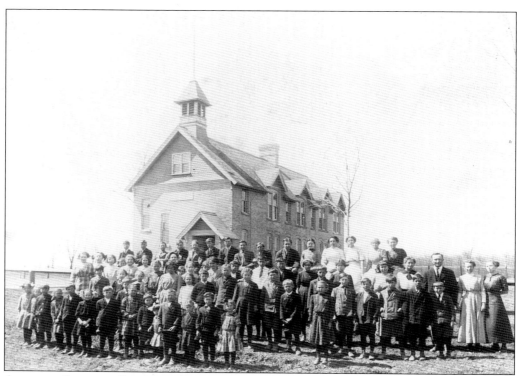

ANOTHER SCENE OF OAKWOOD SCHOOL IN 1910. The second floor was used as the high school from 1888 to 1918. Tuition was 40¢ a week. (Courtesy of Oak Creek Historical Society.)

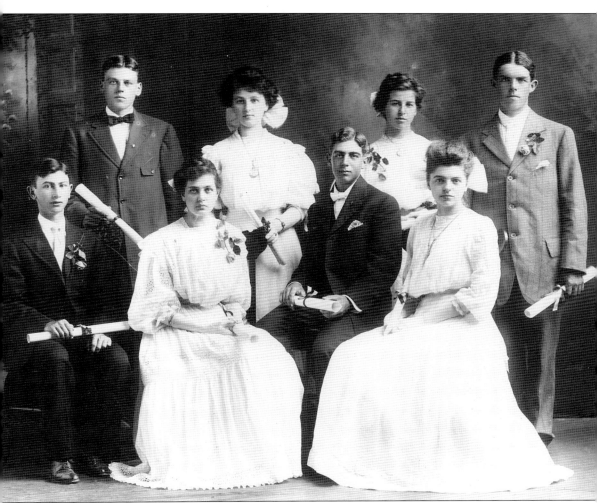

THE GRADUATING CLASS OF OAKWOOD HIGH SCHOOL, 1908. Pictured from left to right are: (seated) Arthur Hahn, Louise Schlitz, Ervin Heyman, and Erma Meyer; (standing) Arthur Goetsch, Irene Warzyn, Lizzie Baden, and Willie Ray. (Courtesy of Violet Mahr.)

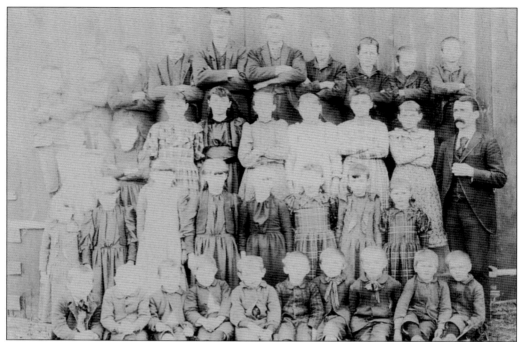

DISTRICT THREE SCHOOL, 1893. Years later the school became known as the Green Lawn School. The teacher is believed to be either Daniel P. Harrigan or John Harrington. (Courtesy of CNI Newspapers.)

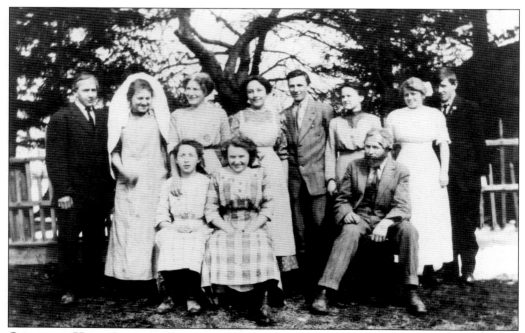

OAKWOOD HIGH SCHOOL "LITERARY SOCIETY," 1912. This was a group of high school students who put on dramas and plays. (Courtesy of Oak Creek Historical Society.)

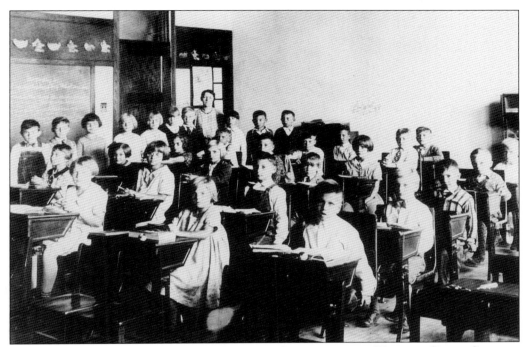

INSIDE THE CLASSROOM FOR A GROUP PHOTO OF STUDENTS FROM HICKORY GROVE SCHOOL, 1931. (Courtesy of Gordon and Dolores Esch.)

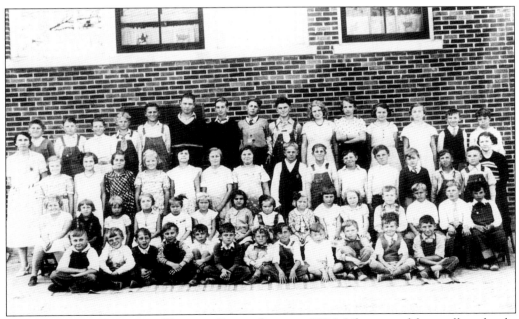

OUTDOOR CLASS PHOTO OF HICKORY GROVE SCHOOL, 1936. Like most of the smaller schools, Hickory Grove would end its classes and eventually be torn down due to consolidation of Oak Creek's grade schools in the 1950s and 1960s. (Courtesy of Gordon and Dolores Esch.)

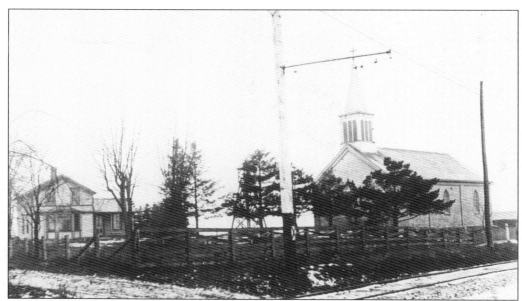

ST. MATTHEW'S CHURCH ON SOUTH CHICAGO ROAD, 1920S. The building to the left is the second rectory. Note the streetcar line running in front of the church. Built in 1860, the church would serve Catholics of the Carrollville area until 1962. (Courtesy of LeRoy and Beulah Meyer.)

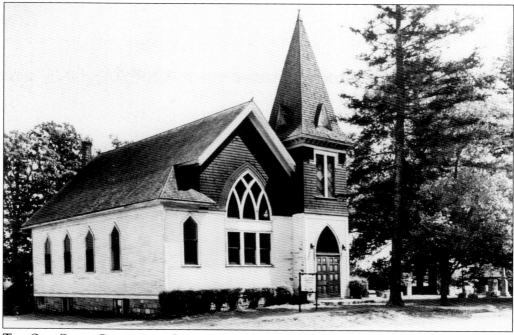

THE OAK CREEK COMMUNITY CHURCH, 1950S. The church was located on South 13th Street, just north of Drexel Avenue. Lightning would strike the church on March 12, 1954, starting a fire that would completely destroy the building. The congregation would build a new church on 13th and Puetz in 1955. (Courtesy of Gordon and Dolores Esch.)

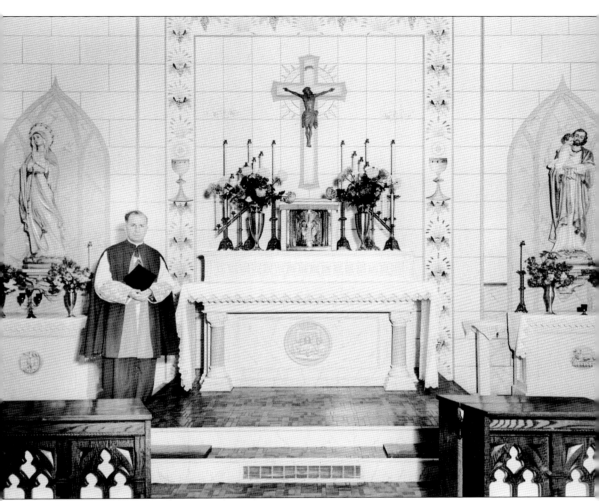

FATHER GEORGE B. RADANDT, STANDING BESIDE THE ALTER OF ST. MATTHEW'S CHURCH, C. 1940S. Father Radandt was St. Matthew's 40th pastor, serving the parish from 1933 to 1956. A restoration project for the church began in the 1980s to bring the "old" church back to the way it looked in the late 19th century. (Courtesy of Oak Creek Historical Society.)

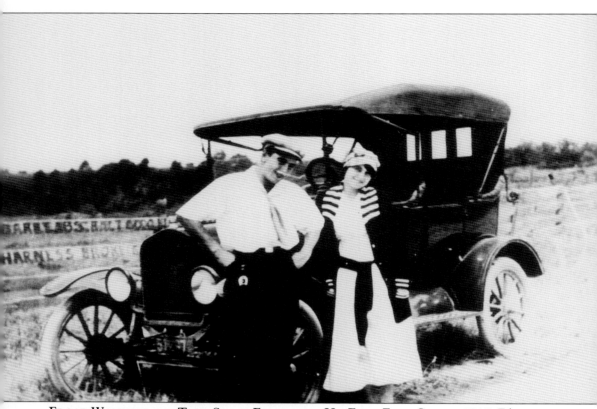

EDGAR WOHLUST AND TWIN SISTER EDNA, WITH HIS FIRST FORD CAR, C. 1919. Edgar was a World War I veteran and a blacksmith in Oak Creek. (Courtesy of LeRoy and Beulah Meyer.)

Four

SPECIAL TIMES AND SPECIAL PLACES

Since Oak Creek was basically a farming community, all members of the family pitched in to help whenever needed. There were, of course, non-farming jobs, but farming or not, there were days you felt would never end. In spite of all the hard work involved, one thing never changes—the sense of togetherness in a small community where people help one another. Neighbors and family members that lived in your same town were still miles away on rough roads. This fact made the leisure times together that much more special. There would be occasions to show off a new vehicle, a new child, or celebrate a special event. Oak Creek had its fair share of unique places to live, work, and play. Many of the old businesses and homes are long gone, and our only way to recall the feelings and emotions of those special times and special places is to view the images that can tell the stories best.

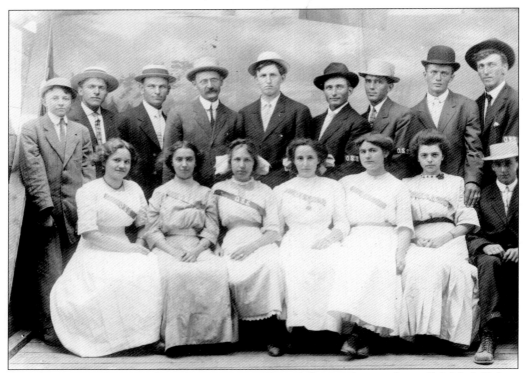

THE OAKWOOD SINGING SOCIETY, C. 1912. From left to right are: (seated) Mabel Halter, Katherine Meyer, Elsie Dorpat, Elsie Halter, Cora Kleinmann, Erma Meyer, and Elmer Honadel; (standing) Elgin Halter, Alfred Meyer, Peter Gerber, Director Dr. Louis Dorpat, Merrill Kleinmann, Henry Mahr, Henry Michel, O. Meyer, and Henry Krohn. (Courtesy of Elroy and Nancy Honadel.)

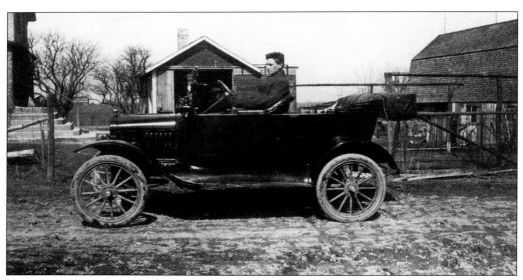

LEON ZIMDARS, DRIVING HIS CAR ON THE ZIMDARS FARM ON OAKWOOD AND HOWELL AVENUE, AROUND THE 1920s. (Courtesy of Oak Creek Historical Society.)

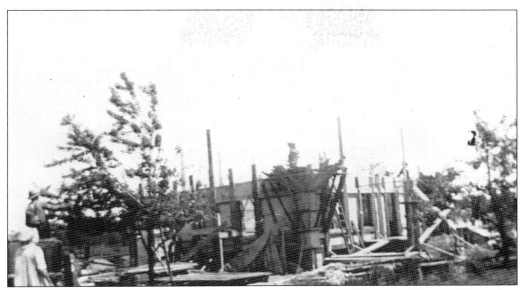

CONCRETE FORMS BEING PUT IN PLACE FOR THE GANTZ "CASTLE HOUSE," LOCATED ON PUETZ ROAD BETWEEN HIGHWAY 32 AND 15TH AVENUE. The Gantz home was believed to be the first home built mostly of concrete in Wisconsin. (Courtesy of Oak Creek Historical Society.)

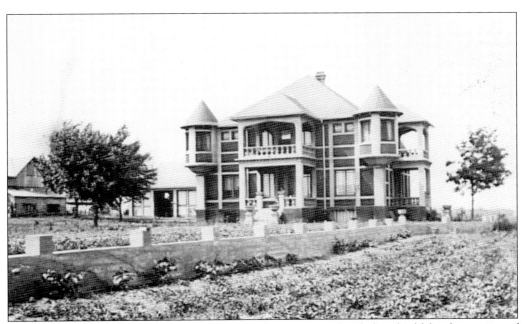

THE GANTZ CONCRETE HOUSE, C. 1920S. Albert Gantz decided to build his home out of concrete after a fire destroyed his original home. The woodwork in his home was made from the walnut trees that grew on his property. After years of neglect, the house was razed in 1991. (Courtesy of Oak Creek Historical Society.)

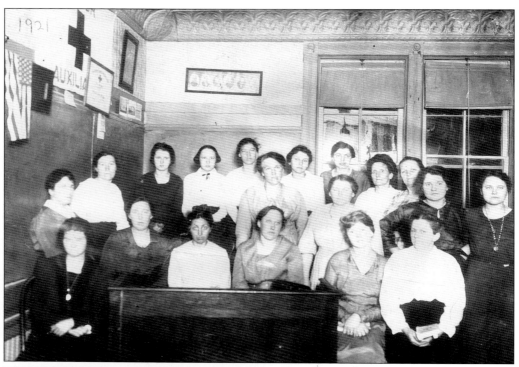

RED CROSS CLASS AT OAKWOOD SCHOOL, AROUND 1921. In the Red Cross class the women learned first aid and the art of bandaging wounds. This became a necessity due to the shortage of doctors in the area. (Courtesy of Oak Creek Historical Society.)

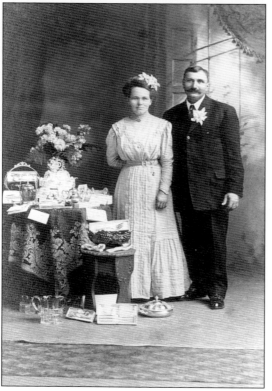

ANNA AND ERNEST WOHLUST'S 25TH WEDDING ANNIVERSARY, 1910. The items to their left were their anniversary gifts. (Courtesy of Oak Creek Historical Society.)

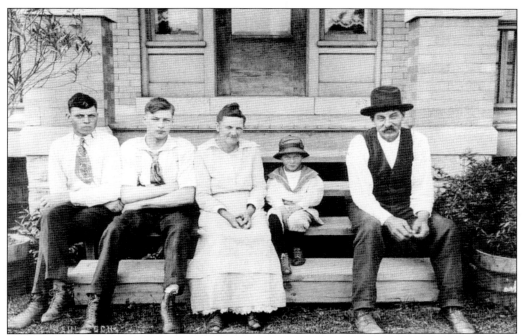

THE VANSELOW FAMILY—ROMAN, GROVER, ELIZABETH, MARLIN AND GUSTAVE. The photo was taken in June 1919. (Courtesy of Duane O. Vanselow.)

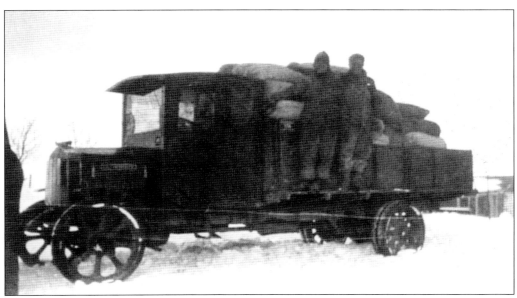

ELROY AND ELMER HONADEL, TAKING A LOAD OF GRAIN TO TOWN IN JANUARY 1919. (Courtesy of Elroy and Nancy Honadel.)

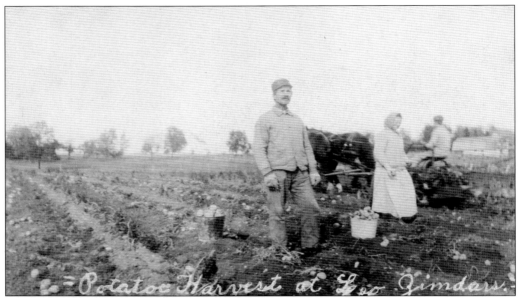

FALL HARVEST. Harvesting potatoes at the Leo Zimdars farm are: Leo, Minnia, and Clarence Zimdars. (Courtesy of Carolyn Haack.)

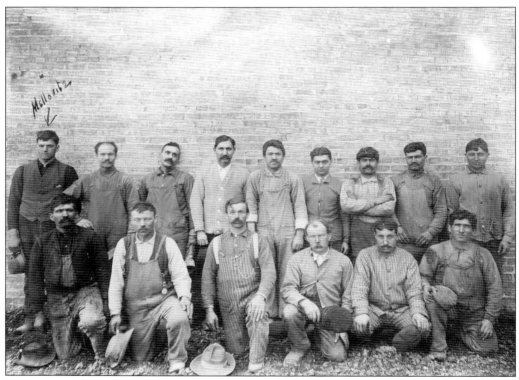

PRESS ROOM WORKERS IN THE UNITED STATES GLUE COMPANY IN CARROLLVILLE, C. 1915. Later the company became known as the Peter Cooper Glue Company. (Courtesy of Robert Morrow.)

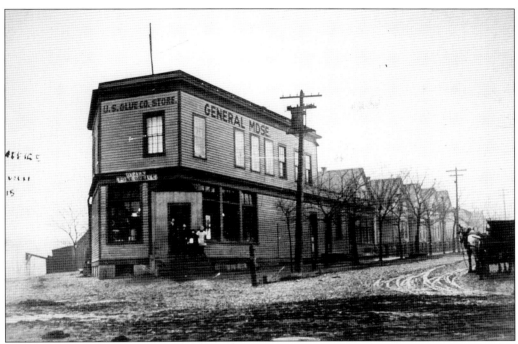

UNITED STATES GLUE COMPANY GENERAL STORE. This is where workers and their families bought needed supplies. The Otjen Post Office was also located in this building. (Courtesy of LeRoy and Beulah Meyer.)

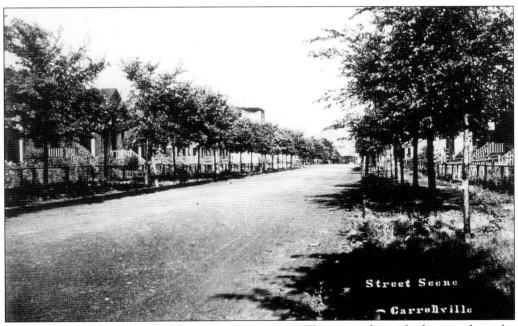

STREET SCENE FROM CARROLLVILLE, AROUND 1915. This scene shows the homes where the employees of the United States Glue Factory and their families lived. (Courtesy of LeRoy and Beulah Meyer.)

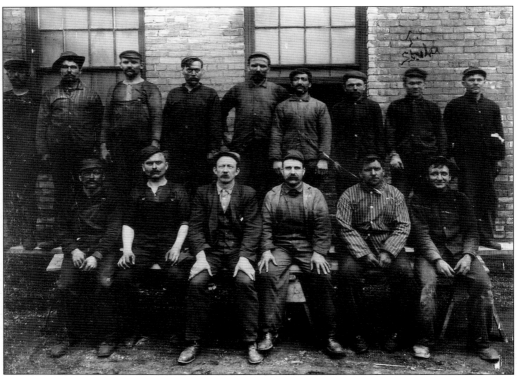

ENGINE AND BOILER ROOM WORKERS FROM THE UNITED STATES GLUE FACTORY. These men would be responsible for running and maintaining the factory's own power plant. (Courtesy of Robert Morrow.)

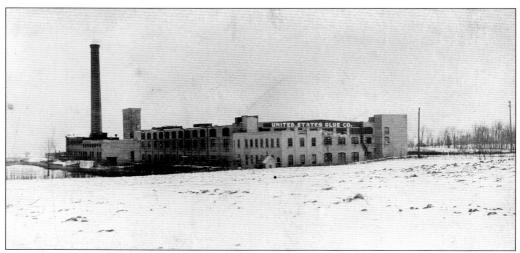

OUTSIDE THE UNITED STATES GLUE FACTORY, AROUND 1910. The glue factory was started when tanners in Wisconsin and surrounding states decided they could make more money turning their tannery by-product into glue rather than sell it to other firms. Cheap land and proximity to Milwaukee and Lake Michigan made Carrollville the location of choice. (Courtesy of Robert Morrow.)

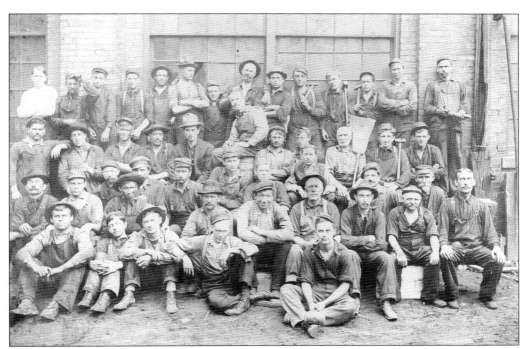

ANOTHER GROUP PHOTO OF UNITED STATES GLUE COMPANY WORKERS, AROUND 1915. When first opened in 1899, the factory had 150 employees, some of whom would work on the two company-owned farms and maintain company-provided employee housing. (Courtesy of Robert Morrow.)

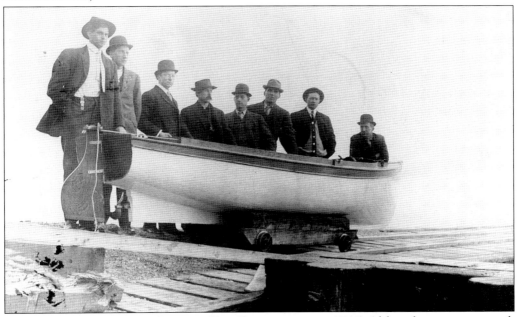

THE UNITED STATES GLUE COMPANY FIRE DEPARTMENT, C. 1915. Although company-owned, this was the only fire department of any sort at the time in the Oak Creek area. (Courtesy of Robert Morrow.)

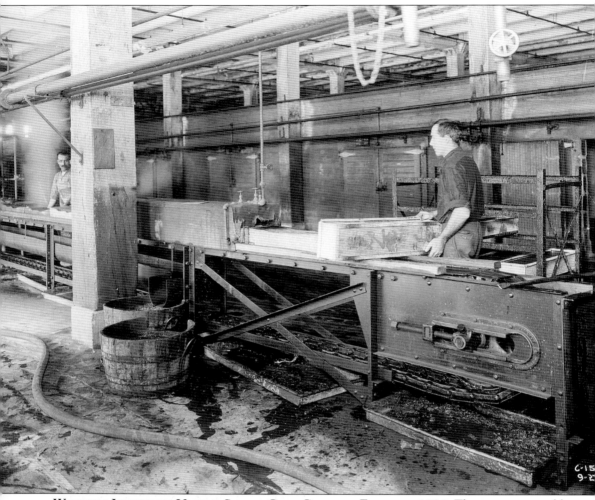

WORKING INSIDE THE UNITED STATES GLUE COMPANY FACTORY, 1920. The company would also add a gelatin operation this year. After being sold to the Peter Cooper Corporation of Gowanda, New York in the early 1930s, two-thirds of the work force would be laid off. (Courtesy of Robert Morrow.)

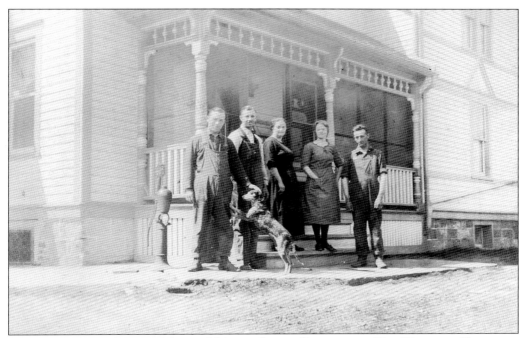

THE HONADELS—GEORGE, ELROY, MOTHER LUCY, CLARA, AND HER HUSBAND ELMER ON THE HONADEL FARM, 1923. (Courtesy of Elroy and Nancy Honadel.)

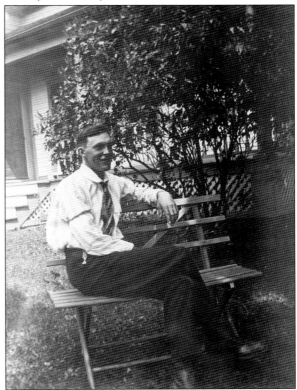

CHARLES MAASS, RELAXING AT HIS FARM ON NICHOLSON ROAD, AROUND 1929. (Courtesy of Oak Creek Historical Society.)

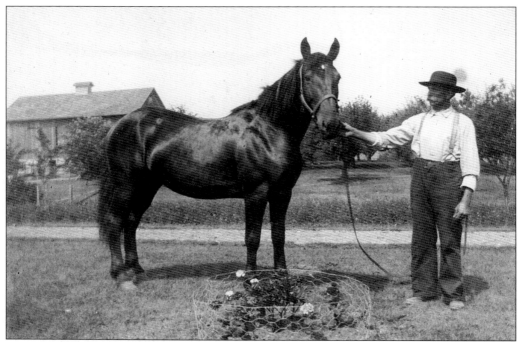

GUSTAVE MILLER ON HIS FARM WITH HIS HORSE SANDY. The Miller farm was located at Howell and Puetz. (Courtesy of Oak Creek Historical Society.)

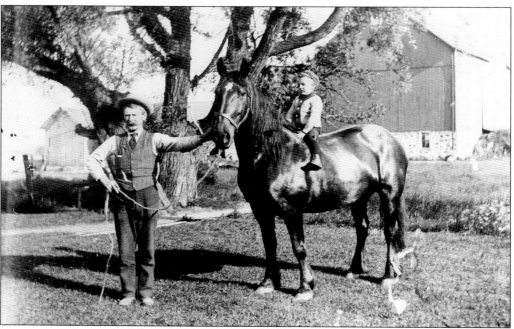

HERMAN (LEFT) AND SON CLARENCE FRANKE. They are enjoying a horse ride on the Franke farm, around South 27th Street and Drexel Avenue. (Courtesy of Oak Creek Historical Society.)

ELROY O. HONADEL, IN A CAR DESCRIBED AS A LOCOMOBILE EIGHT. This photo was taken on July 17, 1924. (Courtesy of Elroy and Nancy Honadel.)

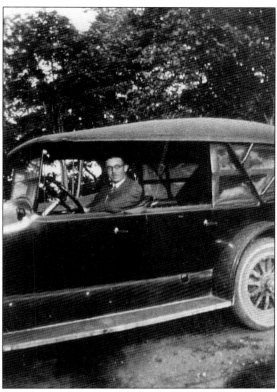

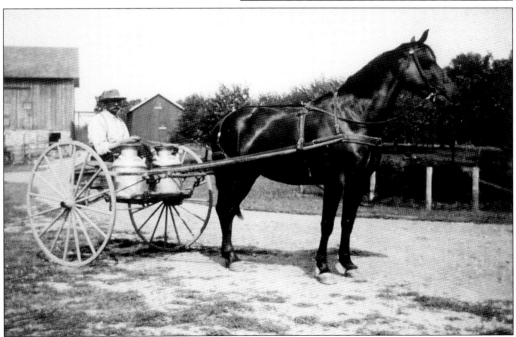

HAULING MILK CANS BY HORSE-DRAWN CART ON THE MEYER FARM, AROUND THE LATE 1920S. (Courtesy of LeRoy and Beulah Meyer.)

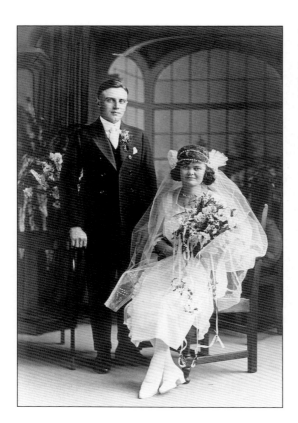

WEDDING PHOTO OF EDGAR AND ELSIE WOHLUST. Edgar owned and worked in one of Oak Creek's eight blacksmith shops. (Courtesy of Oak Creek Historical Society.)

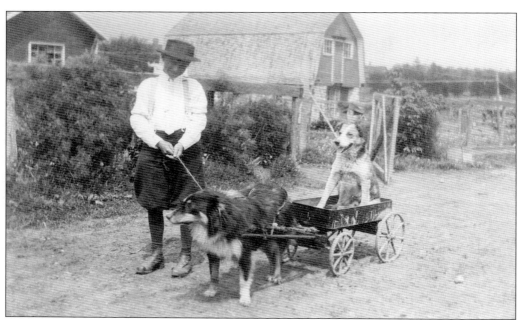

CLARENCE ZIMDARS, HAVING FUN WITH TWO CANINE FRIENDS ON THE ZIMDARS FARM, C. 1915. (Courtesy of Oak Creek Historical Society.)

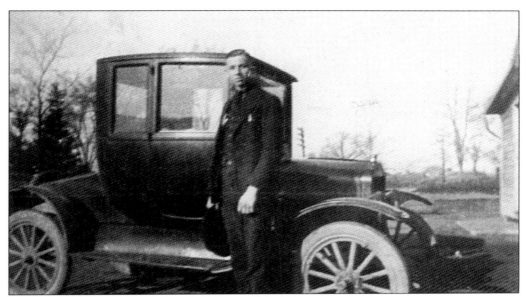

MODEL-T FORD OF ELROY O. HONADEL, EARLY 1920S. (Courtesy of Elroy and Nancy Honadel.)

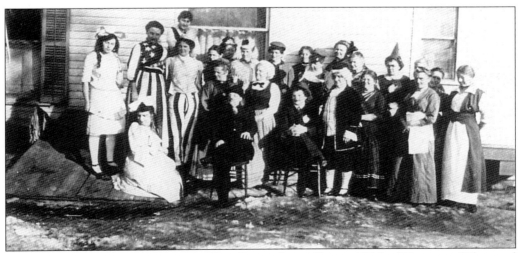

FOURTH OF JULY FESTIVITIES IN THE OAK CREEK AREA, EARLY 1930S. (Courtesy of Elroy and Nancy Honadel.)

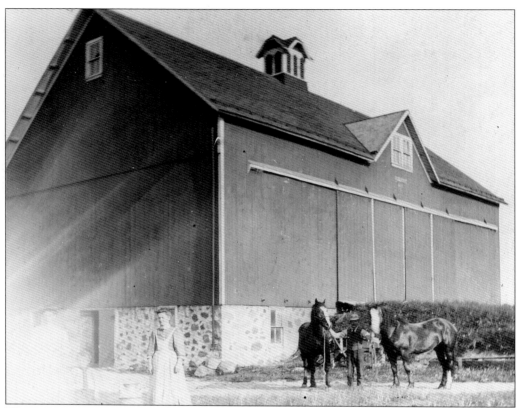

WORKING IN FRONT OF THE FRANKE BARN, C. 1920. Clarence Franke is the young boy, to his right is his mother, and Herman Franke is between the horses. (Courtesy of Oak Creek Historical Society.)

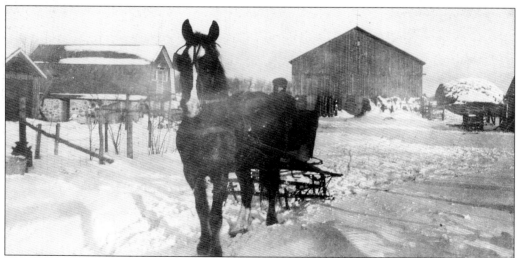

HORSE-DRAWN SLEIGH IN A WINTER SCENE ON THE ZIMDARS FARM NEAR HOWELL AVENUE AND OAKWOOD ROAD. (Courtesy of Oak Creek Historical Society.)

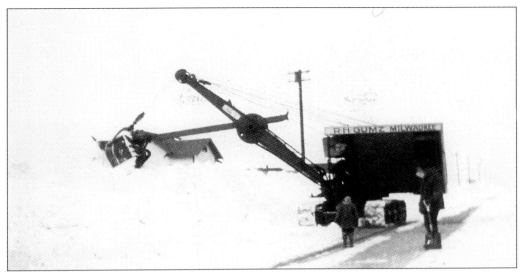

ELROY HONADEL JR. (LEFT), WATCHING SNOW REMOVAL ON HIGHWAY 41 NEAR PUETZ ROAD IN 1936.

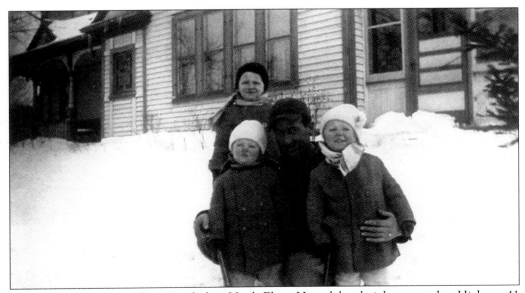

HONADEL HOMESTEAD. Posing with their Uncle Elmer Honadel at their homestead on Highway 41 and Puetz Road are Elroy Honadel Jr. and his twin sisters, LaVaughn and Renee. This photo was taken in the winter of 1937–38. (Courtesy of Elroy and Nancy Honadel.)

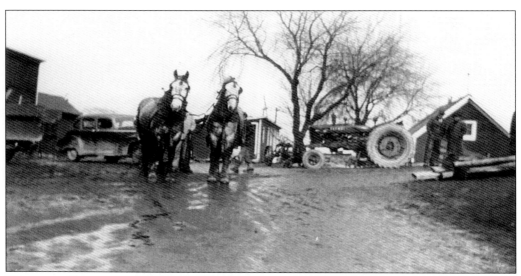

HITCHING HORSES ON THE MAASS FARM, AROUND THE LATE 1930S OR EARLY 1940S. The Maass farm was located on Nicholson Road between Puetz and Ryan. (Courtesy of Oak Creek Historical Society.)

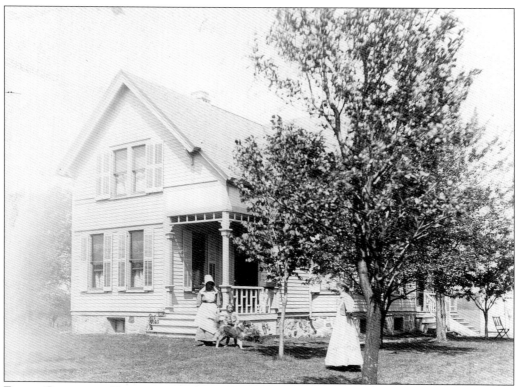

EDNA, CLARENCE, BLINKO, AND ANNE FRANKE, POSING IN FRONT OF THEIR HOME ON A NICE SUMMER DAY. (Courtesy of Oak Creek Historical Society.)

The Maass Family Dog, on a Fence Post on the Family Farm. (Courtesy of Oak Creek Historical Society.)

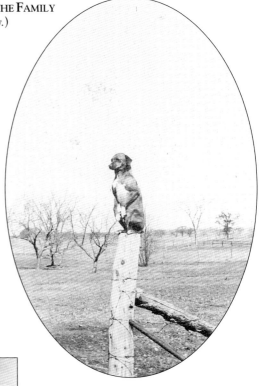

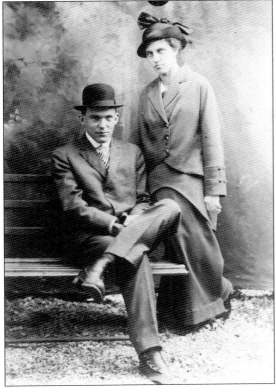

Charles Maass and Bertha Kehe, around the Early 1910s. Charles and Bertha were married in 1917. (Courtesy of Oak Creek Historical Society.)

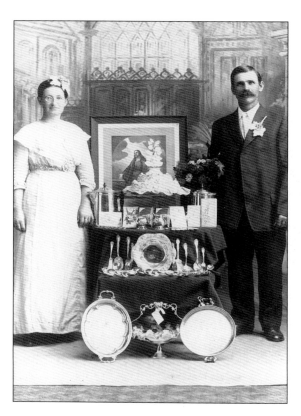

LEO ZIMDARS AND MINNIA ZIMDARS (NEE LAST) ON THEIR 25TH WEDDING ANNIVERSARY IN 1912. (Courtesy of Carolyn Haack.)

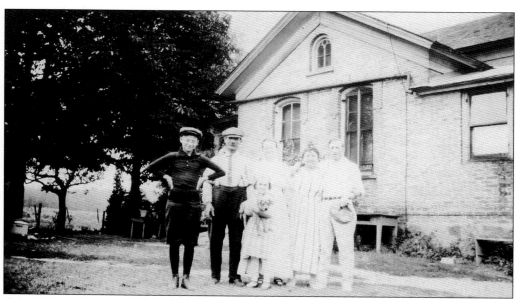

THE FRANK ZIMDARS HOME ON OAKWOOD ROAD, AROUND THE 1920S. (Courtesy of Carolyn Haack.)

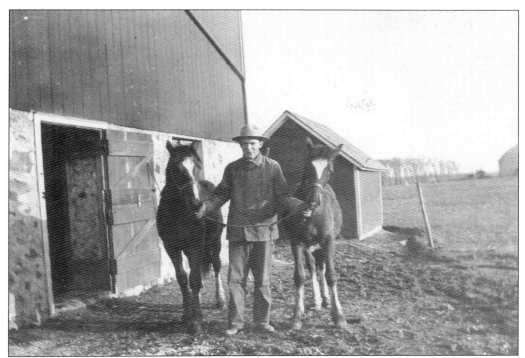

CHARLES MAASS, TENDING TO TWO OF HIS HORSES ON HIS FARM. (Courtesy of Oak Creek Historical Society.)

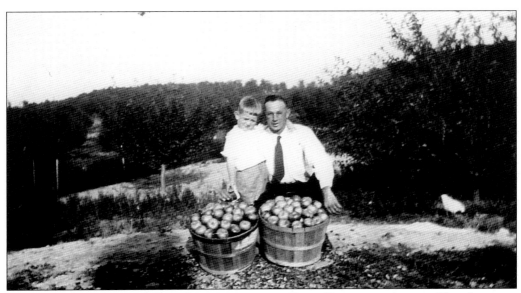

ELROY HONADEL SR. AND SON GEORGE WITH THE FIRST BUSHEL OF APPLES. The photo was taken in the fall, around 1927 or 1928. (Courtesy of Elroy and Nancy Honadel.)

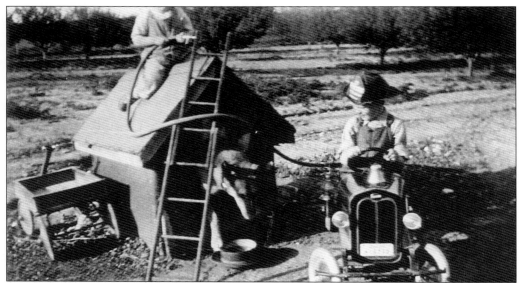

GEORGE AND ELROY HONADEL JR., PLAYING ON THE FAMILY FARM IN 1934. Note the fire truck pedal car—a very popular toy for decades. (Courtesy of Elroy and Nancy Honadel.)

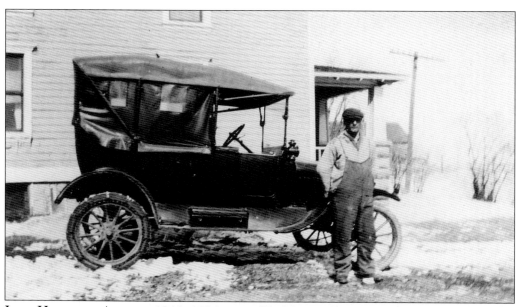

JOHN HEYMANN, AROUND 1918–1920, WITH HIS MODEL-T, AT THE 7300 BLOCK OF SOUTH HOWELL AVENUE. (Courtesy of Eleanore and Alfred Hauerwas.)

WEDDING PHOTO OF CHARLES AND BERTHA MAASS, 1917. Both were nearly life-long residents in the Oak Creek area. (Courtesy of Carolyn Haack.)

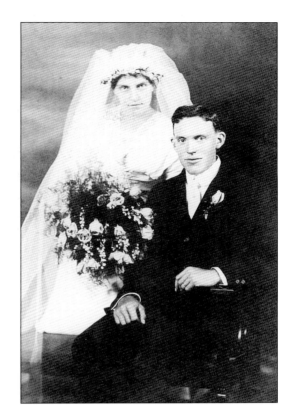

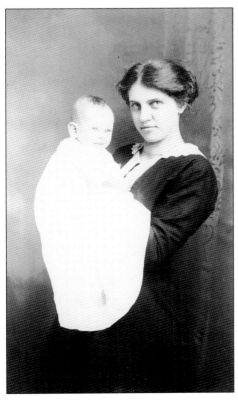

BERTHA MAASS, POSING WITH HER DAUGHTER GLADYS, BORN JANUARY 21, 1927. (Courtesy of Carolyn Haack.)

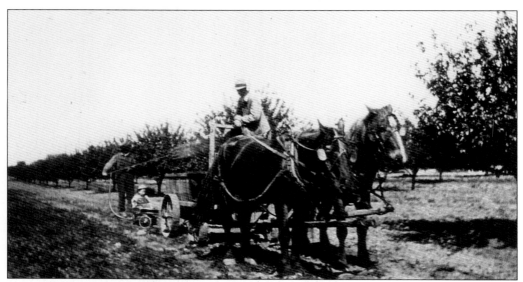

SPRAYING THE APPLE ORCHARD TREES, USING HORSE-DRAWN EQUIPMENT, ON THE HONADEL FARM IN 1932. (Courtesy of Elroy and Nancy Honadel.)

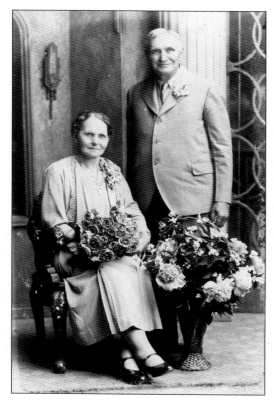

GOLDEN ANNIVERSARY PHOTO OF ERNST AND ANNA WOHLUST (NEE VANSELOW). They were married on June 25, 1885. (Courtesy of Oak Creek Historical Society.)

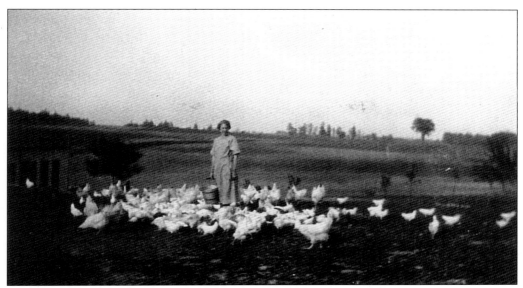

CLARA HONADEL, TENDING TO A FLOCK OF CHICKENS ON THE HONADEL FARM IN THE 1930s. (Courtesy of Elroy and Nancy Honadel.)

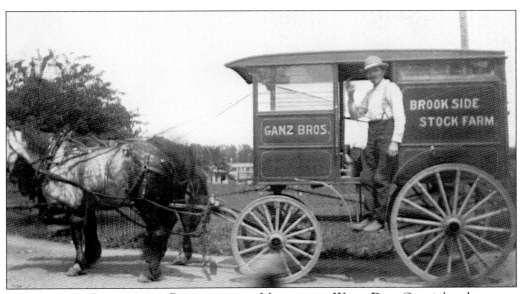

ALBERT GANZ, POSING FOR A PICTURE IN THE MIDDLE OF A WORK DAY. Ganz is best known as the man who had the "Castle House" built on Puetz Road (see photo in this chapter). (Courtesy of Oak Creek Historical Society.)

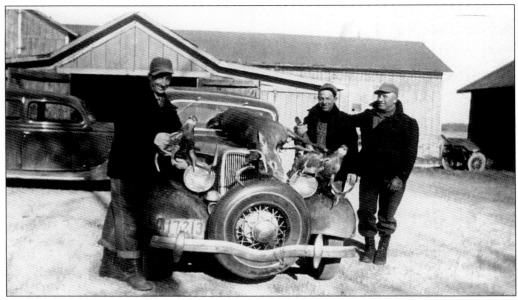

ELMER AND GEORGE HONADEL WITH WALTER HAHN (LEFT TO RIGHT), LATE 1930s. These men show the results of their participation in the long-standing tradition of Wisconsin whitetail deer hunting. (Courtesy of Elroy and Nancy Honadel.)

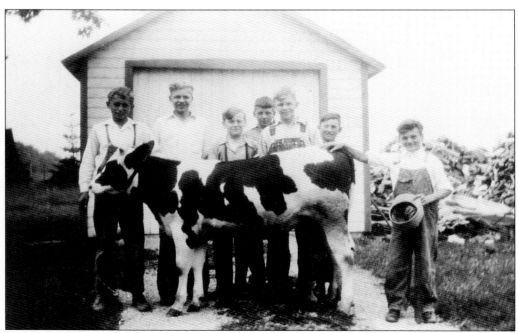

A PROUD GROUP OF YOUNG BOYS POSING WITH A HOLSTEIN CALF ON THE MAHR FARM ON SOUTH 27TH STREET IN THE 1930s. (Courtesy of Violet Mahr.)

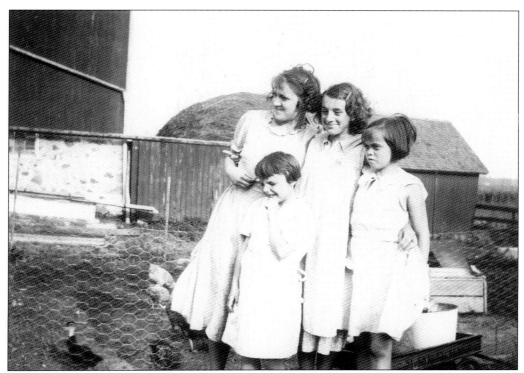

HAZEL ANNA WILKE, EVELYN KEHE, LARINA WOHLUST, AND GLADYS MAASS, IN FRONT OF THE CHARLES MAASS FARM, MID-1930S. (Courtesy of Oak Creek Historical Society.)

APPLE ROADSIDE MARKET ON SOUTH 27TH STREET. Elroy Honadel Jr., exchange student from Holland, and Vernon Honadel are pictured here. The photo was taken in the fall of 1948 or 1949. (Courtesy of Elroy and Nancy Honadel.)

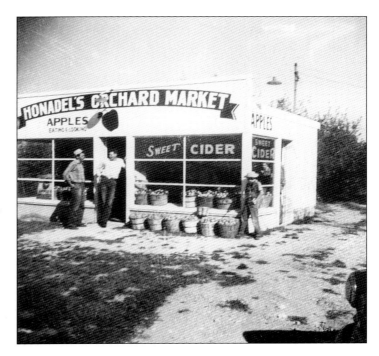

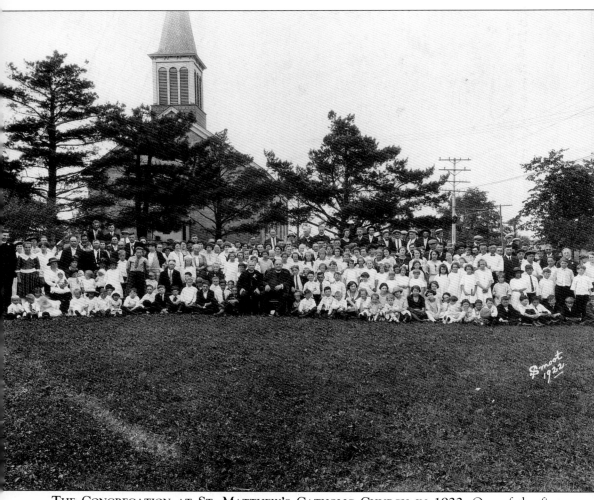

THE CONGREGATION AT ST. MATTHEW'S CATHOLIC CHURCH IN 1922. One of the first churches established in the Oak Creek area, it has provided for the spiritual needs of many generations of families and holds a special place in the city's history. (Courtesy of Oak Creek Historical Society.)

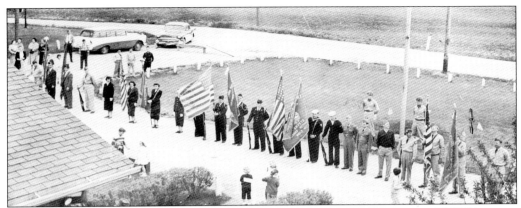

MEMORIAL DAY SERVICE IN MAY OF 1957 AT THE OELSCHLAEGER DALLMANN VFW POST ON SHEPARD AVENUE. (Courtesy of CNI Newspapers.)

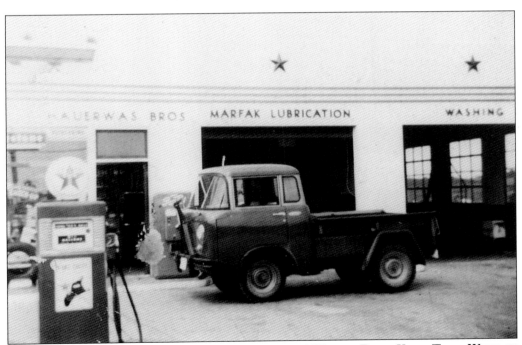

THE HAUERWAS BROTHERS TEXACO STATION, IN 1957, THE FIRST YEAR THEY WERE IN BUSINESS. The station was located on the corner of Howell and Puetz Road, going out of business in 1988. (Courtesy of Eleanore and Alfred Hauerwas.)

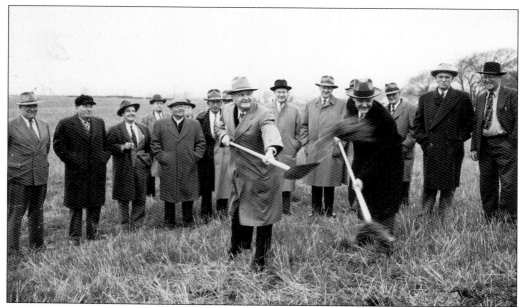

GROUNDBREAKING CEREMONY FOR THE WISCONSIN ELECTRIC POWER COMPANY'S OAK CREEK POWER PLANT ON MAY 4, 1951. (Courtesy of Oak Creek Historical Society.)

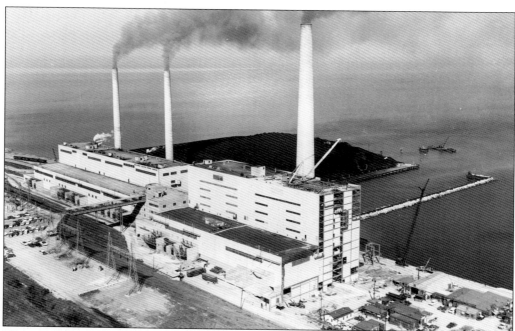

WISCONSIN ELECTRIC POWER COMPANY'S OAK CREEK POWER PLANT, SHORTLY AFTER GOING ON LINE AROUND 1953. The tax revenue generated by this power plant would inadvertently spark a strong-handed battle with Milwaukee to annex Oak Creek. (Courtesy of Oak Creek Historical Society.)

Memorial Day Ceremonies at the Oelschlaeger Dallmann VFW Post 434, 1958. Seen here are: Flag Handler LeRoy A. Schmidt; firing squad (from the left) Delbert Sonnabend, Willard Gaida, and George and William Wetzel. (Courtesy of CNI Newspapers.)

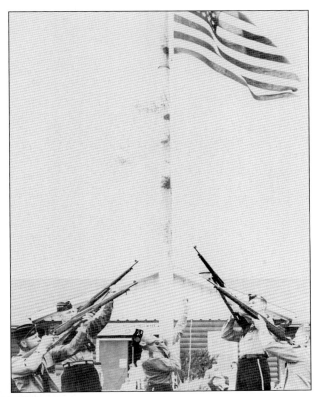

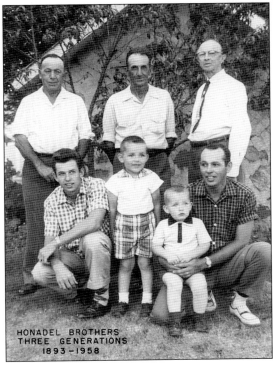

The Honadel Brothers. Pictured from left to right, they are: (standing) George, Elmer, and Elroy; (first row) Vernon (son of Elroy Sr.), Dean (son of Elroy Jr.), Elroy Jr., and (on knee) Mark (son of Elroy Jr.). (Courtesy of Elroy and Nancy Honadel.)

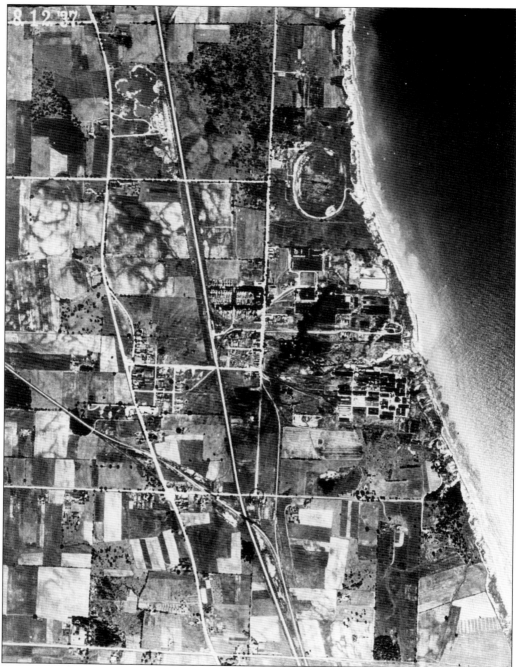

AN AERIAL VIEW OF THE EASTERN PORTION OF OAK CREEK ON AUGUST 12, 1937. The oval shape near Lake Michigan in the upper right corner is the remains of the South Milwaukee Speedway, which by this time was abandoned for several years. Below the race track are the buildings of Carrollville's numerous industries, including the DuPont Chemical Company and the Peter Cooper Corporation. The remainder of the view demonstrates how much farmland was in Oak Creek at this time. (Courtesy of Oak Creek Historical Society.)

Five

THE LAY OF THE LAND

As with all towns on the move, Oak Creek's progress changed its landscape. Dirt roads were paved, barns came down, and farmlands became subdivisions. Although some larger open areas are still around, it is difficult to believe now that the entire town was very much one farm after another. The large buildings and big companies were located to the north, in South Milwaukee, and to the east in Carrollville until the 1950s. But the fact remains that hundreds of acres of farm soil made way for single-family homes and eventually businesses both large and small. The move from township to city would forever change the lay of the land. You can feel a certain appreciation for the drive it must have taken to work such large pieces of land, and the stress of depending on nature to provide the essentials for a good crop. Looking back, it is somewhat sad to think that the family farm and apple orchards would be no more, as Oak Creek started to make the transition from rural town to growing suburb.

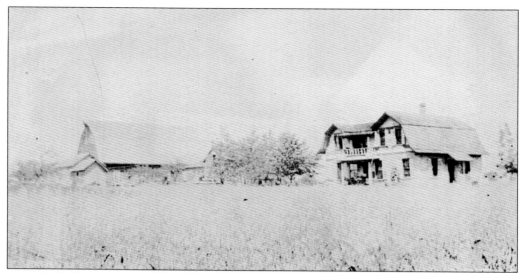

The Ganz Farmstead on Puetz Road, Between Highway 32 and 15th Avenue, Early 1900s. The farmhouse on the right was destroyed by fire, and Albert Ganz would have the all-concrete "Castle House" built in its place in 1911. (Courtesy of Oak Creek Historical Society.)

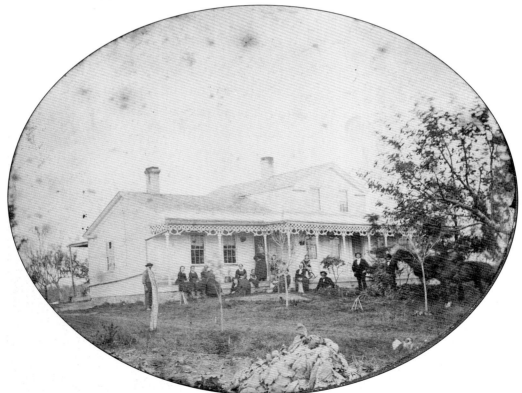

The Honadel Homestead in a Scene Taken on October 24, 1870. The house was located near what is now South 27th Street and Puetz.

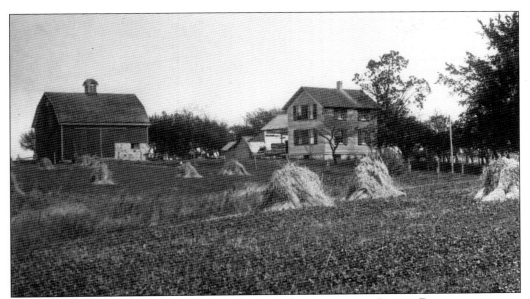

Summer Scene from the Schumacher Farm on Nicholson Road, Probably in the 1930s. (Courtesy of Oak Creek Historical Society.)

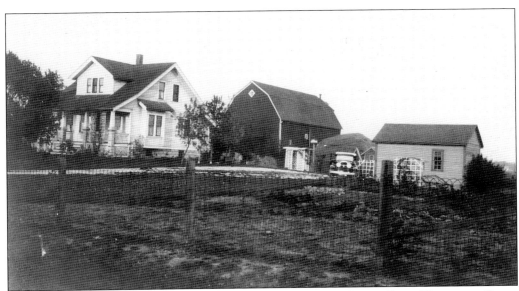

The Charles and Bertha Maass Farm on Nicholson Road, Just North of Ryan Road, in the 1930s. (Courtesy of Oak Creek Historical Society.)

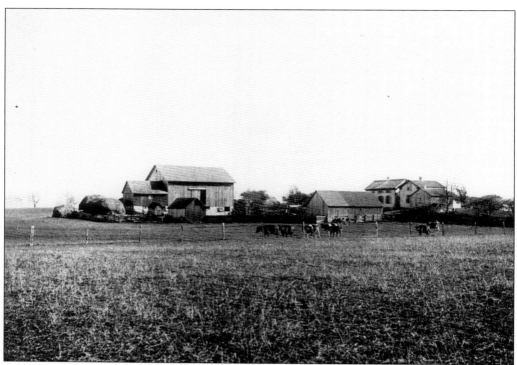

THE CHRIS SCHERBARTH FARM, LOCATED ON PUETZ ROAD. The farm would be wiped out by the construction of Interstate 94 in 1963. (Courtesy of Oak Creek Historical Society.)

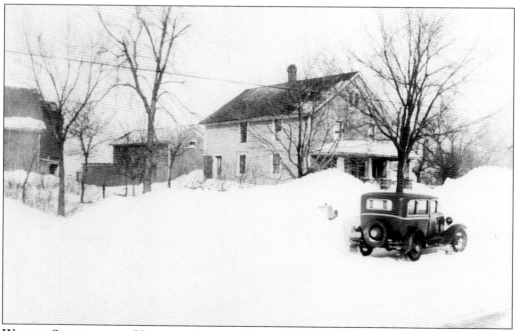

WINTER SCENE AT THE HEYMANN FAMILY HOMESTEAD, NEAR THE 7300 BLOCK OF HOWELL AVENUE, IN THE 1920s. (Courtesy of Eleanore and Alfred Hauerwas.)

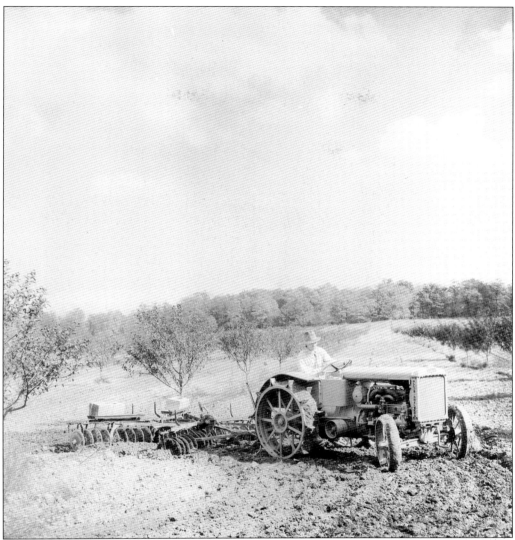

ELROY O. HONADEL SR., WORKING THE LAND BY THE APPLE ORCHARD IN 1930. The original apple tree plantings were done in 1924 on one-third of a quarter section of the Honadel homestead property. The Honadels sold apples from their orchard until the fall of 1997.

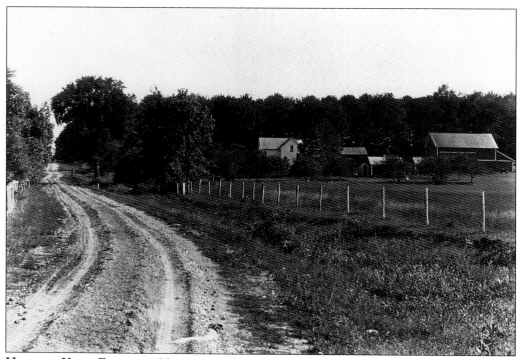

Herman Kehe Farm on Nicholson Road, About 1/3 Mile South of Oak Creek in Caledonia, Just across the Milwaukee-Racine County Line. (Courtesy of Carolyn Haack.)

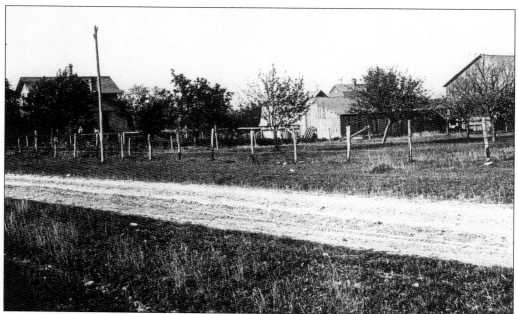

The Leo Zimdars Farm on Howell Avenue and Oakwood Road. This farmland is now a golf course. (Courtesy of Carolyn Haack.)

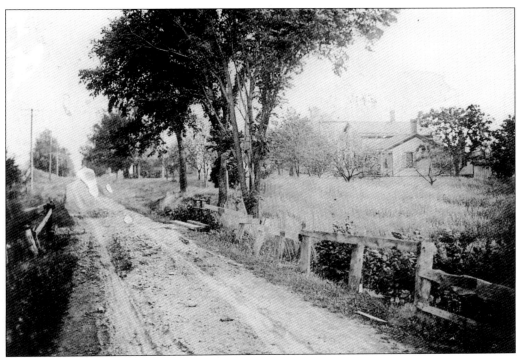

THE HAUERWAS HOMESTEAD AT 8841 SOUTH 13TH STREET IN THE EARLY 1920S. (Courtesy of Eleanore and Alfred Hauerwas.)

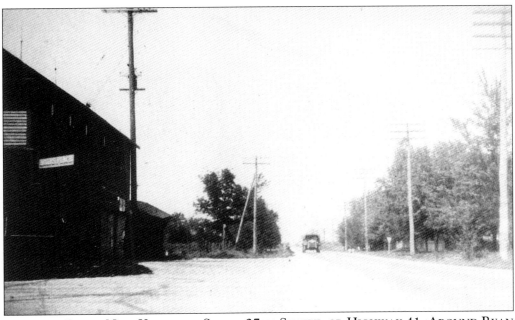

KILBOURN ROAD, NOW KNOWN AS SOUTH 27TH STREET, OR HIGHWAY 41, AROUND RYAN ROAD IN THE 1930S, LOOKING NORTH. (Courtesy of LeRoy and Beulah Meyer.)

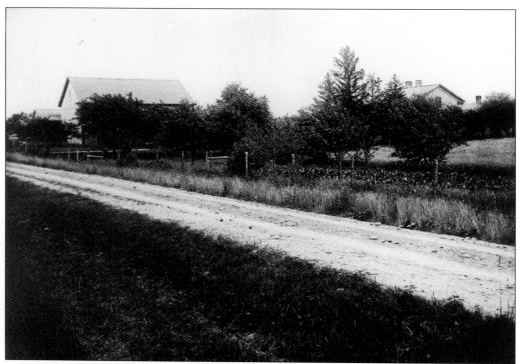

THE TROST HOMESTEAD, 2205 WEST RYAN ROAD, 1912. The house was built in 1859 out of local brick. (Courtesy of Oak Creek Historical Society.)

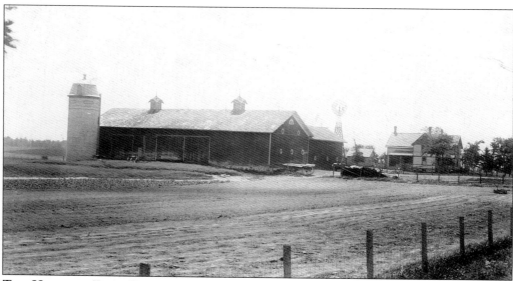

THE HONADEL FARM BUILDINGS, WITH THE HOME IN THE BACKGROUND. The buildings were located on the northeast corner of Kilbourn Road (South 27th Street) and Puetz Road. (Courtesy of Elroy and Nancy Honadel.)

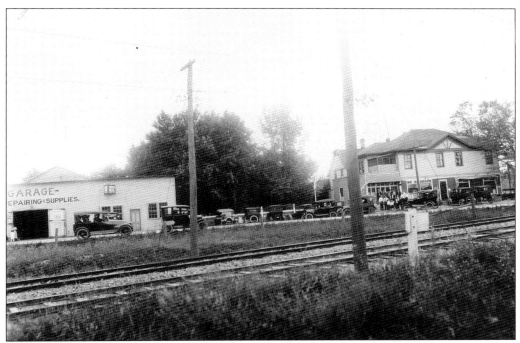

NEAR THE CORNER OF RAWSON AND HOWELL AVENUES, IN THE EARLY 1930S. Inter-urban tracks are visible in the foreground. (Courtesy of Oak Creek Historical Society.)

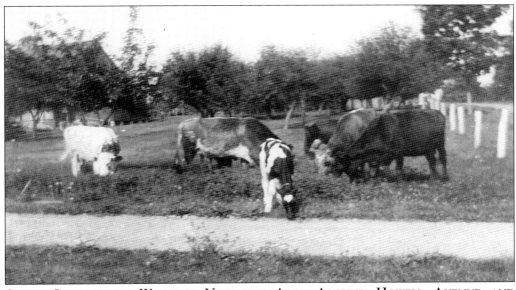

COWS, GRAZING ON WHAT IS NOW THE AREA AROUND HOWELL AVENUE AND PUETZ ROAD, THE FORMER GUSTAVE MILLER FARMSTEAD. (Courtesy of Oak Creek Historical Society.)

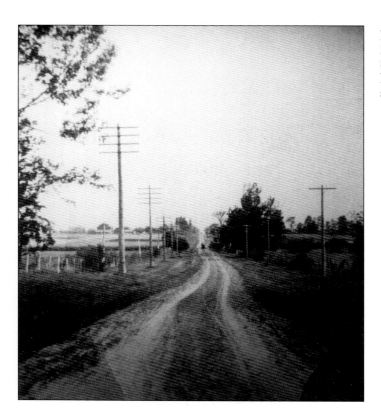

KILBOURN ROAD (SOUTH 27TH STREET), LOOKING SOUTH FROM RYAN ROAD. (Courtesy of LeRoy and Beulah Meyer.)

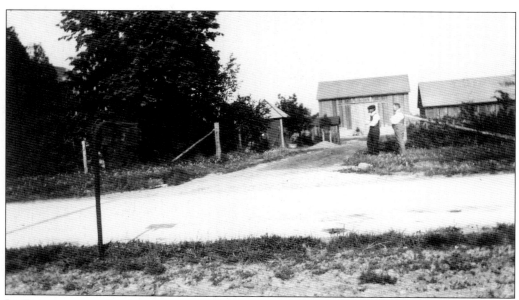

IN FRONT OF THE ZIMDARS FARM, AS SEEN FROM OAKWOOD ROAD, IN THE 1930S. (Courtesy of Carolyn Haack.)

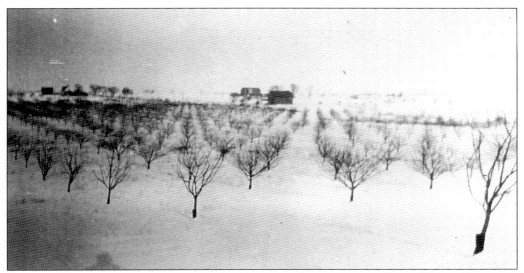

ELROY O. HONADEL'S APPLE ORCHARD, IN 1926, SHOWING THE FIRST TREES PLANTED. (Courtesy of Elroy and Nancy Honadel.)

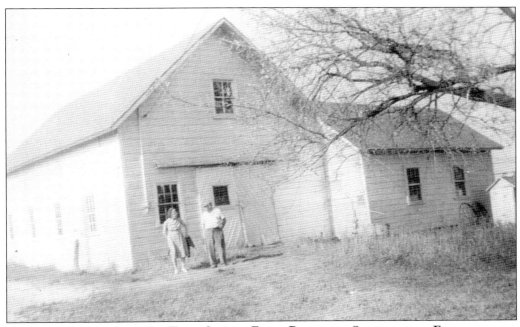

EDGAR WOHLUST AND HIS TWIN SISTER, EDNA RADUENZ, STANDING IN FRONT OF THE WOHLUST BLACKSMITH SHOP IN THE SPRING OF 1964. (Courtesy of Neal Raduenz.)

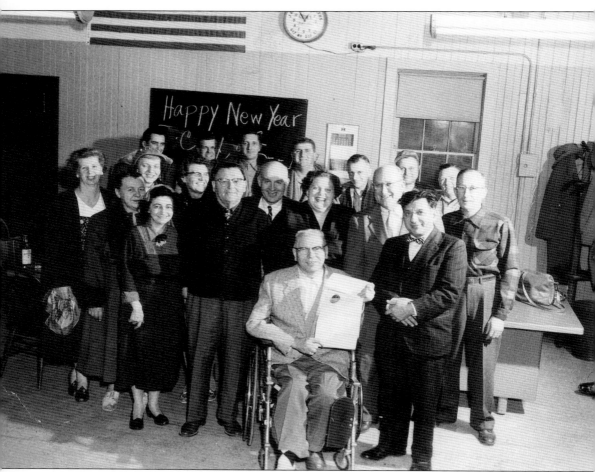

The City of Oak Creek. Early in the morning, on December 16, 1955, town officials posed for a historic photo shortly after returning from Madison with the certificate of incorporation. This photo was taken in the old town hall located on Howell Avenue and Puetz Road. (Courtesy of LaVerne Gutknecht.)

Six

BECOMING A CITY

Oak Creek's transition from town to city would happen only after a staunch battle of wits to fight off an annexation effort from Milwaukee. The new Wisconsin Electric power plant stirred Milwaukee's interest in taking over Oak Creek due to a special law regarding utility tax money. The state required utility companies to return 65 percent of this tax revenue to the community that it was located in. But the part-time town officials, many of whom were farmers by trade, fought off the big city's attempt by first drafting, and then having the state pass what became known as "The Oak Creek Law." The law allowed towns surrounding the city of Milwaukee to incorporate if they met a certain population and assessed land value requirements. Secondly, they beat Milwaukee by managing to derail the big city's effort to stop the incorporation by forcing Oak Creek's officials into a legal quagmire. But defeating Milwaukee's bid to annex was only the start of some of the problems the new city would face. Big companies were moving into the area, and with the benefits came the headaches of adding sewer, water, schools, and increased traffic to accommodate the new employers. Now we can look back and really appreciate the work that went into becoming a city, and how those that laid the ground work made Oak Creek what it is today.

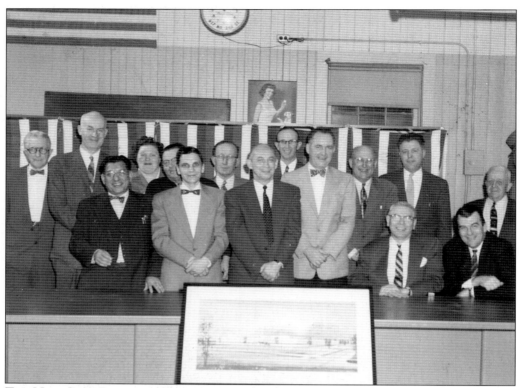

THE NEW CITY OFFICIALS, PROUDLY STANDING BEHIND THE ARCHITECT'S RENDITION OF THE NEW A.C. SPARK PLUG PLANT THAT WOULD BE BUILT IN OAK CREEK. This photo was taken in the town hall on Howell and Puetz. (Courtesy of LaVerne Gutknecht.)

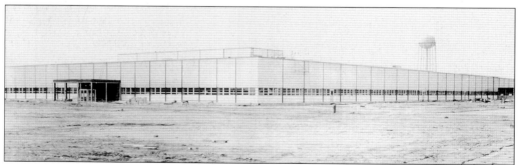

A.C. SPARK PLUG PLANT, IN APRIL 1957, BEFORE CONSTRUCTION WAS COMPLETE. This building occupied 225,000 square feet. The plant is still in operation today and is located on the corner of Howell and Drexel Avenues. (Courtesy of CNI Newspapers.)

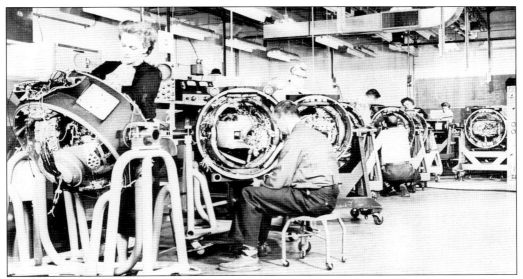

INSIDE THE A.C. SPARK PLUG PLANT, EARLY 1958. The workers are building parts for the missile guidance system for the United States Air Force Thor intermediate range ballistic missiles. (Courtesy of CNI Newspapers.)

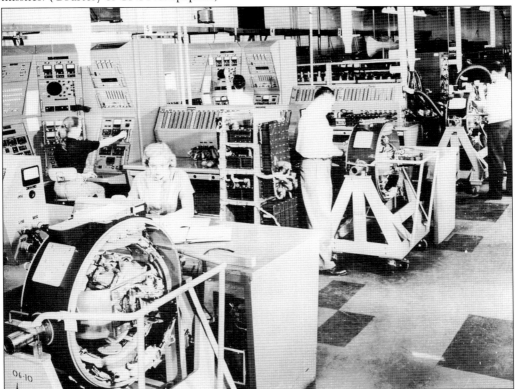

INSIDE A.C. SPARK PLUG, SHOWING THE ACHIEVER INTERNAL GUIDANCE SYSTEMS DOING A PRE-FLIGHT CHECK TO SIMULATE ACTUAL WIRING IN A MISSILE. (Courtesy of CNI Newspapers.)

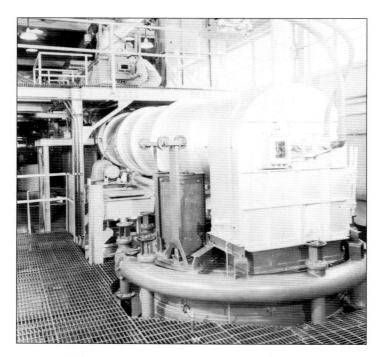

A Scene Inside the Allis Chalmers Pilot Plant in Carrollville, Showing a Rotary Kiln, Which was Used for Metal Processing. It completed heat treating of metal pellets. (Courtesy of CNI Newspapers.)

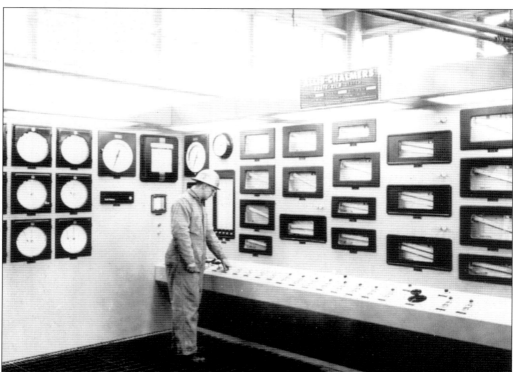

The Master Control Panel, Inside the Allis Chalmers Plant. This panel monitored temperature, flow, and static pressure in their processes. (Courtesy of CNI Newspapers.)

The 1957 Uniform of the Local Force, Shown by Sergeant Lawrence Prochnow. The department assumed responsibility for the law enforcement in the city in January 1957. Originally, the police department was in the vacated Hillside School on Ryan Road. At first the officers had to use their own cars. That changed a few weeks later when the city-ordered vehicles arrived. (Courtesy of CNI Newspapers.)

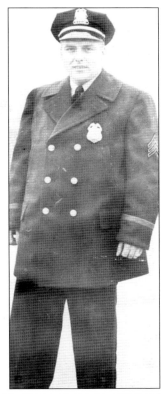

The Humble Beginnings of the Oak Creek Pictorial. The *Pictorial* was established in 1956, Oak Creek's first full year as a city. This building was located on the southeast corner of Howell and Ryan Road. (Courtesy of CNI Newspapers.)

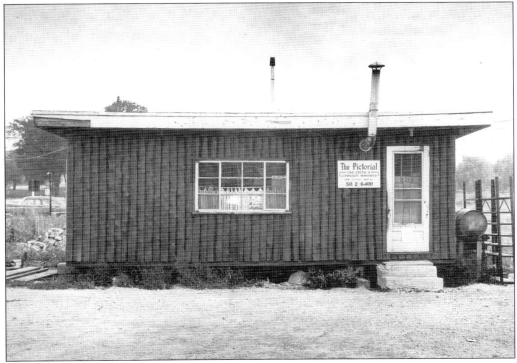

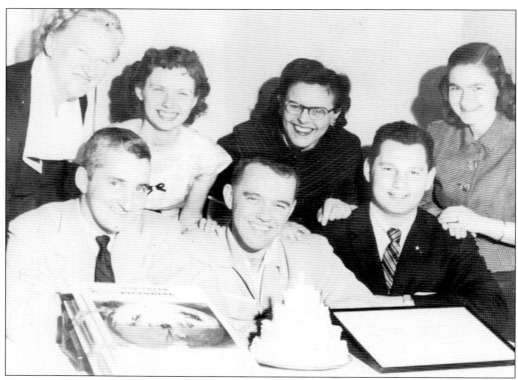

THE ONE YEAR ANNIVERSARY OF THE OAK CREEK PICTORIAL. The staff, from left to right, were: Lois Wolfe, Esther Stolpa, Catherine Jochum, Vernie Smith, Gene Comiskey, Duane Dunham, and Don Stolpa. Under Dunham's leadership, this business would eventually grow to 21 local newspapers known as Community Newspapers Incorporated. (Courtesy of CNI Newspapers.)

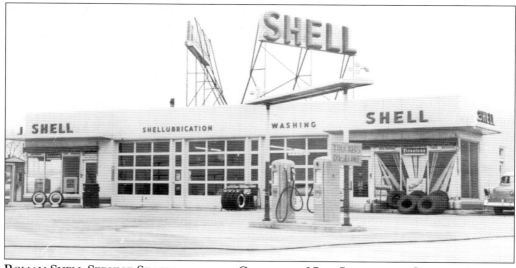

ROMAN SHELL SERVICE STATION, ON THE CORNER OF 27TH STREET AND COLLEGE AVENUE, 1957. (Courtesy of CNI Newspapers.)

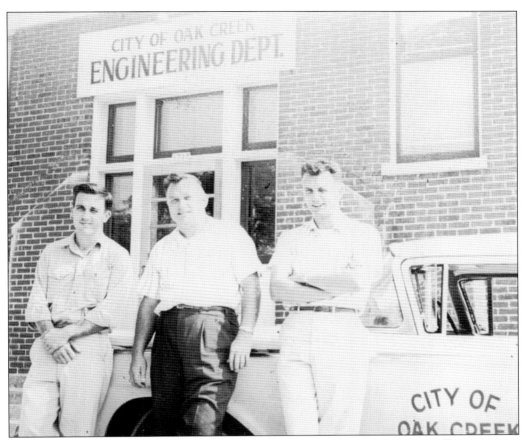

THE OAK CREEK ENGINEERING DEPARTMENT, 1958, OUTSIDE OF THE REFURBISHED OAKWOOD ROAD SCHOOL LOCATED ON 1717 EAST OAKWOOD ROAD. Shown here, from left to right, are: Roger Harris (engineering aide), Richard Hay (city engineer), and Donald Pedo (assistant city engineer). The City Engineering Department was responsible for addressing zoning, sewage, drainage, and water problems in the city. (Courtesy of CNI Newspapers.)

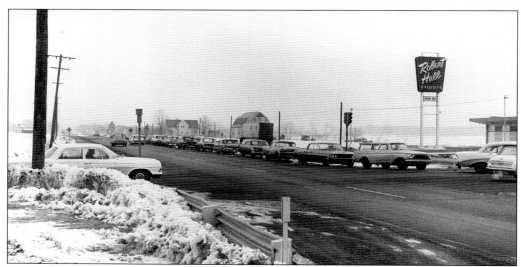

A VIEW NORTH ON 27TH STREET AT DREXEL IN THE EARLY 1960S. This next series of photos is from a traffic study done to examine where improvements would be needed to accommodate the increase in vehicle traffic due to the big companies that moved into Oak Creek. (Courtesy of Oak Creek Historical Society.)

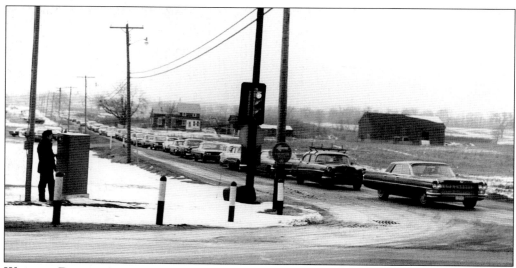

WEST ON DREXEL AVENUE AT HOWELL AVENUE IN THE LATE AFTERNOON. (Courtesy of Oak Creek Historical Society.)

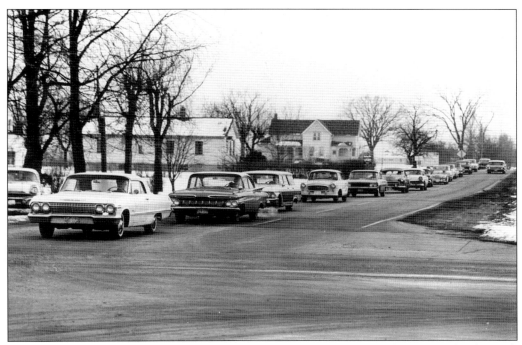

NORTH ON 13TH STREET AT RAWSON AVENUE IN MID AFTERNOON. (Courtesy of Oak Creek Historical Society.)

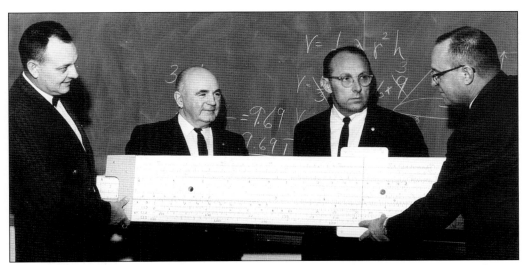

A GIANT SLIDE RULE, PRESENTED TO THE OAK CREEK HIGH SCHOOL, DONATED BY GLENN SUNDERLAND, DIRECTOR OF EDUCATION AND TRAINING FOR A.C. SPARK PLUG. Pictured from left to right are: Weldon Aydelotte (math teacher), Frank Keller (superintendent of schools), Walter J. Mountin (principal), and Glenn Sunderland. (Courtesy of CNI Newspapers.)

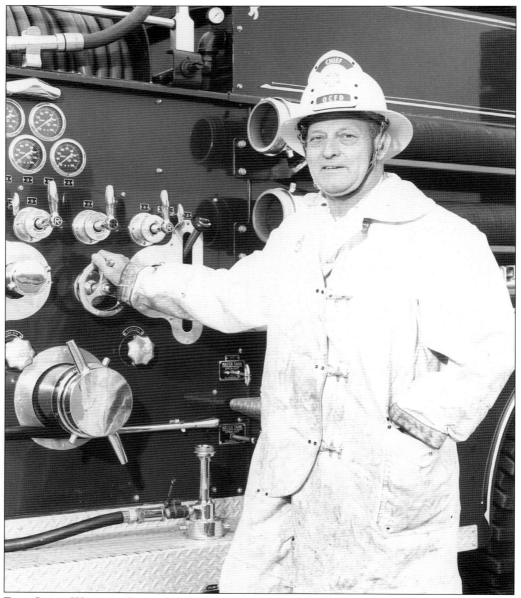

FIRE CHIEF WILLIAM GRADL'S 25TH ANNIVERSARY PHOTO, FOR WORKING FOR THE TOWN AND CITY OF OAK CREEK. When this photo was taken, Mr. Gradl had been a fire chief for the city of Oak Creek for three of those years. This picture was taken in 1964. (Courtesy of CNI Newspapers.)

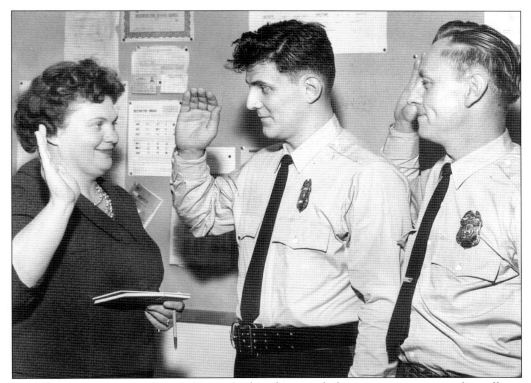

NEW SERVANTS TO THE CITY. LaVerne Gutknecht, city clerk, swears in two new police officers in November 1964. The officer on the left is Derreld Lanctot, and Richard Holmberg is on the right. (Courtesy of CNI Newspapers.)

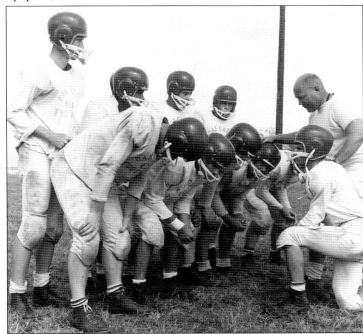

HEAD COACH RON HENRIKSEN, WITH THE OAK CREEK HIGH SCHOOL FOOTBALL TEAM, IN THE FALL OF 1964. The previous year the team had won the Parkland Conference Championship. (Courtesy of CNI Newspapers.)

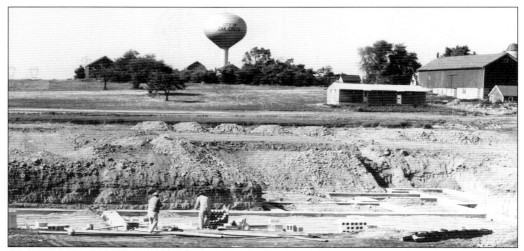

CONSTRUCTION OF OAK CREEK'S FIRST BOWLING ALLEY, LOCATED AT 7501 SOUTH HOWELL AVENUE. The 20-lane alley was built in July of 1965. (Courtesy of CNI Newspapers.)

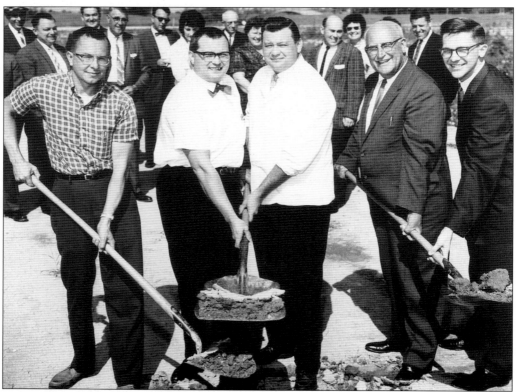

GROUNDBREAKING OF THE OAK BROOK SHOPPING CENTER, JULY 1965. The new shopping center is located on the corner of South Howell Avenue and Ryan Road. Pictured here is (on the left) Marvin Knuth (general contractor), William and Ken Weinhold, Mayor Art Abendschein, and Dr. John Alles. The Weinholds set up their supermarket in the center, and Dr. Alles opened up his dental office in the center.

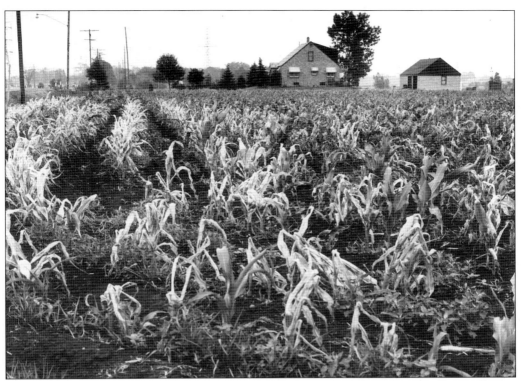

Crop Damage from an Unusual Mid-Summer Frost, July 1965, along Puetz Road, West of Pennsylvania Avenue. (Courtesy of CNI Newspapers.)

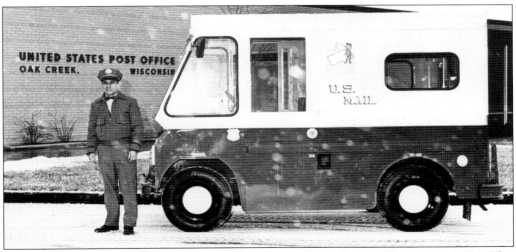

Postman, Standing in Front of the Oak Creek Post Office, November 1964. This modern facility opened in the fall of 1961 and consolidated the last of the small post offices in the Oak Creek area. (Courtesy of CNI Newspapers.)

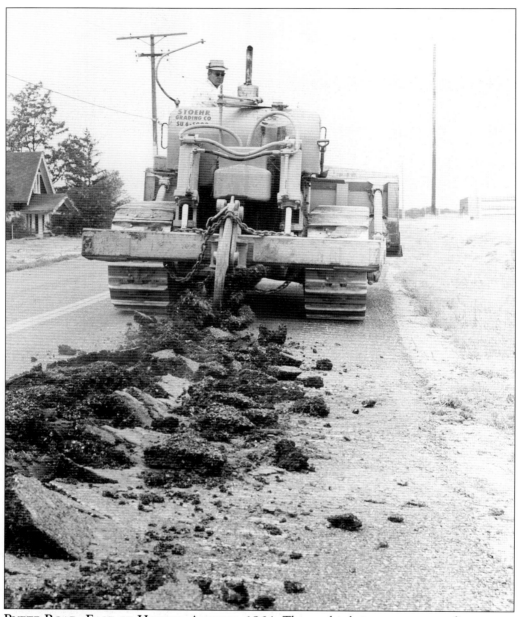
PUETZ ROAD, EAST OF HOWELL AVENUE, 1964. The road is being torn up as a first step to reconstruction that would turn it into a boulevard. (Courtesy of CNI Newspapers.)

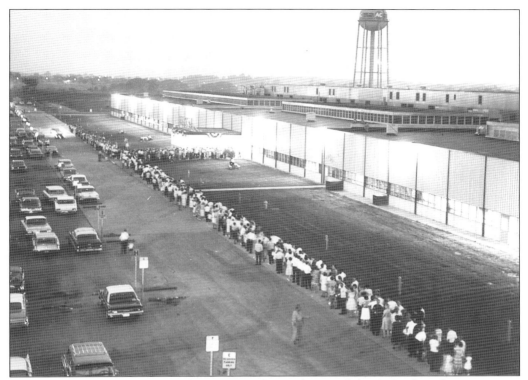

A.C. Spark Plug Plant. In July 1964, 30,000 people toured the A.C. plant during an open house held there. (Courtesy of CNI Newspapers.)

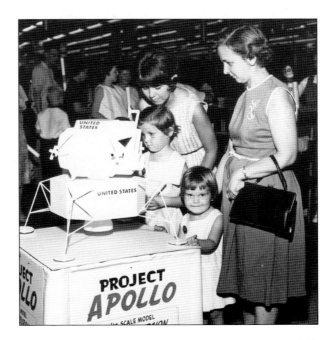

Inside the A.C. Plant, During the Open House. Visitors were able to view the missile guidance systems and the Apollo and Lunar Modules Systems. (Courtesy of CNI Newspapers.)

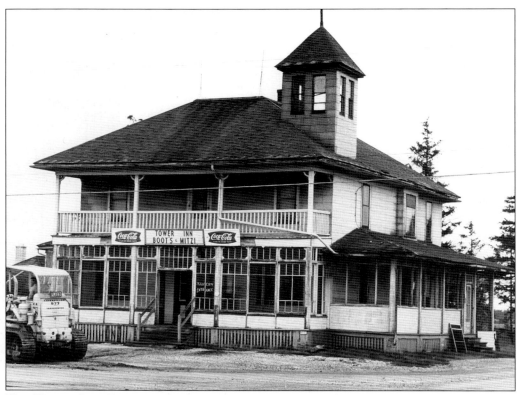

THE TOWER INN, LOCATED ON 13TH AND RYAN ROAD. This was just before it was razed to make room for the Interstate 94 interchange on Ryan Road. (Courtesy of CNI Newspapers.)

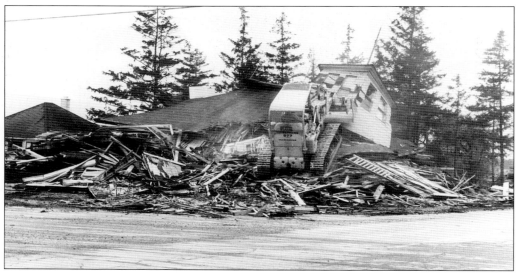

THE TOWER INN, AFTER IT WAS RAZED IN AUGUST 1964. The owners of the Inn were Mr. and Mrs. John Shew, better known to their friends and customers as Boots and Mitzi. The building was originally constructed sometime between 1880 and 1900. In 1910 it was run by Adam Hauerwas. (Courtesy of CNI Newspapers.)

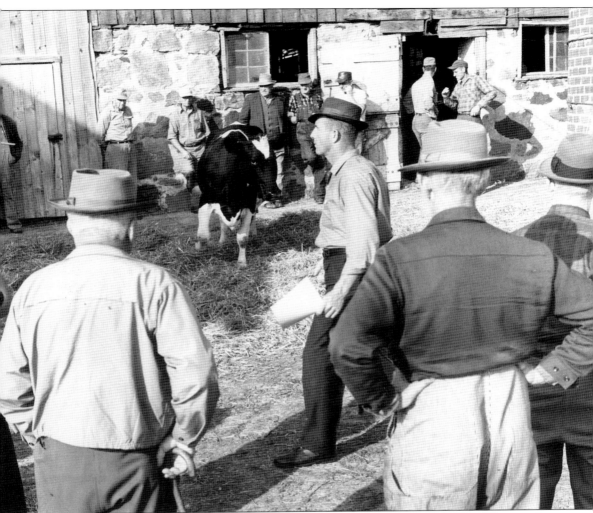

ONE OF THE LAST DAIRY HERDS IN OAK CREEK. The cows are being sold at an auction on the Royal Arsand farm on 10539 South Howell Avenue. This marked the end of the farm's 45 years of dairy farming. This photo was taken in October 1964. (Courtesy of CNI Newspapers.)

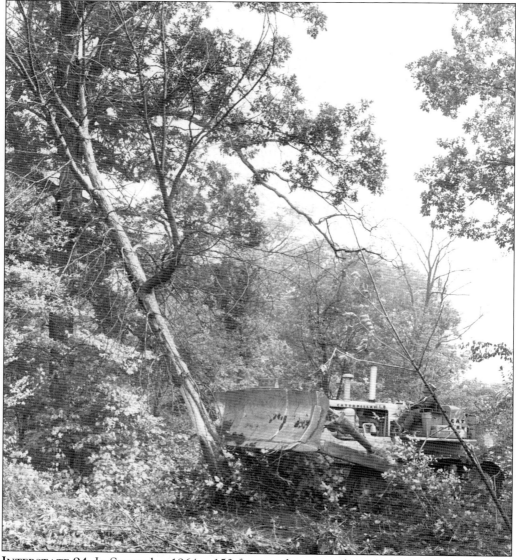
INTERSTATE 94. In September 1964, a 150-foot swath was cut through the dense woods on the eastern section of the Alfred Meyer farm to make room for the Interstate 94 freeway project. (Courtesy of CNI Newspapers.)

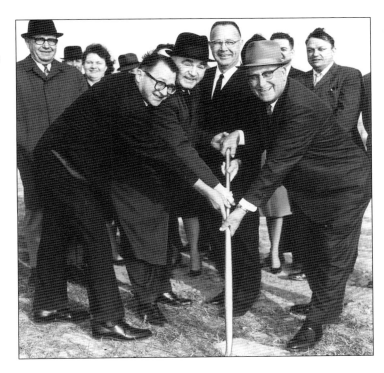

GROUNDBREAKING FOR THE CEDAR HILLS SCHOOL ON OAK CREEK'S NORTHWEST SIDE, MAY 1965. Pictured from left to right are: Alfred H. Zarse (architect), Frank Keller (superintendent of Oak Creek schools), Harold Schmidt (president of the board of education), and Mayor Abendschein. (Courtesy of CNI Newspapers.)

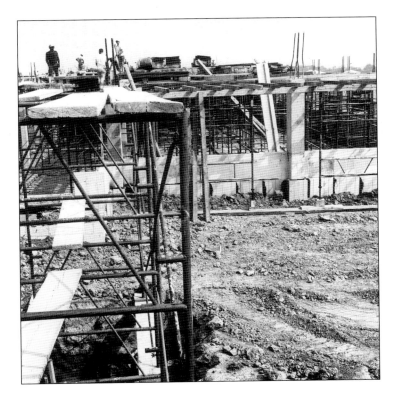

CONSTRUCTION OF THE NEW CEDAR HILLS ELEMENTARY SCHOOL. This school was built to accommodate the growing number of children moving into the Oak Creek area. The photo was taken in July 1965. (Courtesy of CNI Newspapers.)

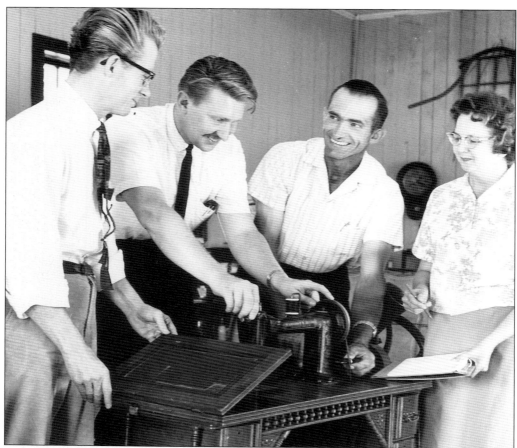

THE OAK CREEK HISTORICAL SOCIETY. The Wisconsin State Historical Society helped the Oak Creek Historical Society in arranging artifacts in the new Oak Creek Historical Society building, which is the former Oak Creek Town Hall. Pictured from left to right are: Charles Knox (exhibit curator from the state historical society), Richard Horn (research curator from the state historical society), Henry Mahr (president of the Oak Creek Historical Society, and Mrs. Curtis Brassaw (the Oak Creek Historical Society secretary). Henry Mahr was instrumental in establishing the Oak Creek Historical Society by saving the town hall from being razed when a new city hall was being constructed on the same site. Mr. Mahr helped raise the funds to move the old town hall to its new home as part of the Oak Creek Historical Society Complex. (Courtesy of CNI Newspapers.)

Two Visitors to the Oak Creek Historical Society in 1964, Taking a Closer Look at One of the Many Interesting Artifacts. (Courtesy of CNI Newspapers.)

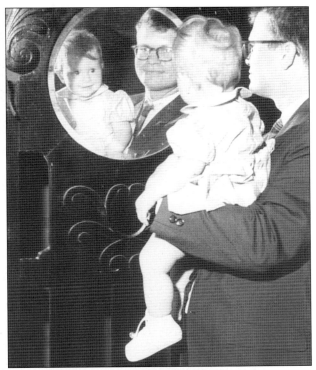

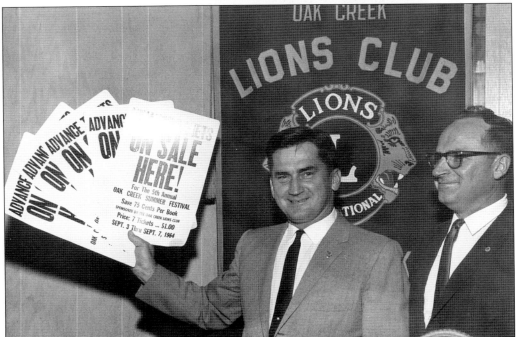

The Oak Creek Lions Club Kick-Off Dinner for the Summer Festival, 1964. The festival, which started in 1959, continues to be an annual Labor Day weekend tradition. (Courtesy of CNI Newspapers.)

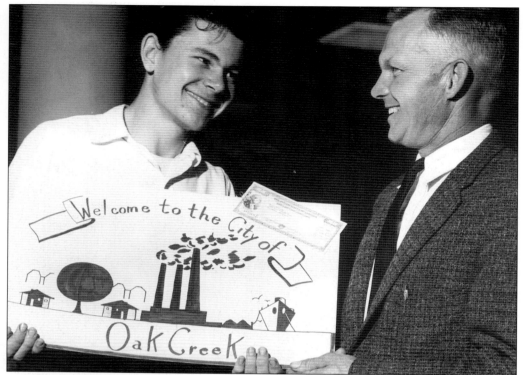

WELCOME TO OAK CREEK. In 1964, the City of Oak Creek held a contest in which Oak Creek High School students made suggestions for a sign near Interstate 94 for visitors entering the city. Rodger Malcom won the contest and is shown receiving his prize from the president of the chamber of commerce, LeRoy Meyer. (Courtesy of CNI Newspapers.)

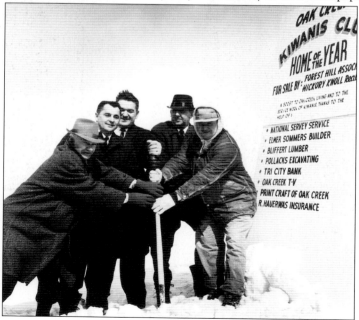

GROUNDBREAKING FOR A NEW HOUSE BEING CONSTRUCTED ON EAST GROVELAND DRIVE, TO FINANCE THE OAK CREEK KIWANIS CLUB COMMUNITY ACTIVITIES. Pictured from left to right are: Herman A. Hamann, Joseph Janicek (committee chairman), Norb Theine (president), Alderman Toivo Kuivanen, and Elmer Sommers (builder). (Courtesy of CNI Newspapers.)

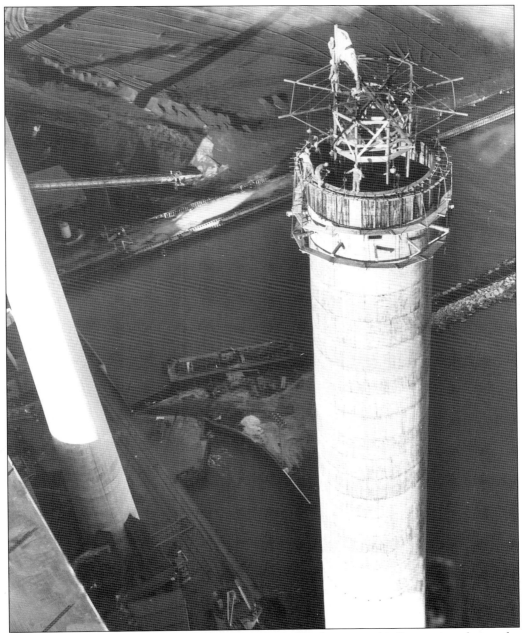

WISCONSIN ELECTRIC OAK CREEK POWER PLANT. Workers got a bird's-eye view during the new construction at the plant. At the time of this photo in 1965, the plant had a capacity of 1,340,000 kilowatts. It consumed 2.7 million tons of coal a year, and more than 7 tons a day. That year Wisconsin Electric's total investment in the power plant was $166 million. (Courtesy of CNI Newspapers.)

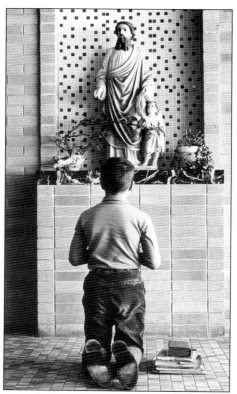

A Young Boy, Praying in St. Matthews School on Chicago Road. The new church and school was completed in 1962. (Courtesy of CNI Newspapers.)

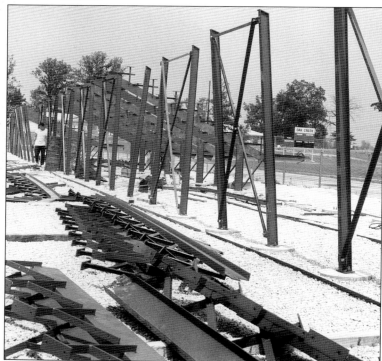

Construction of the Bleachers at the Oak Creek High School in 1964. The first classes were held at the school in the fall of 1961. (Courtesy of CNI Newspapers.)

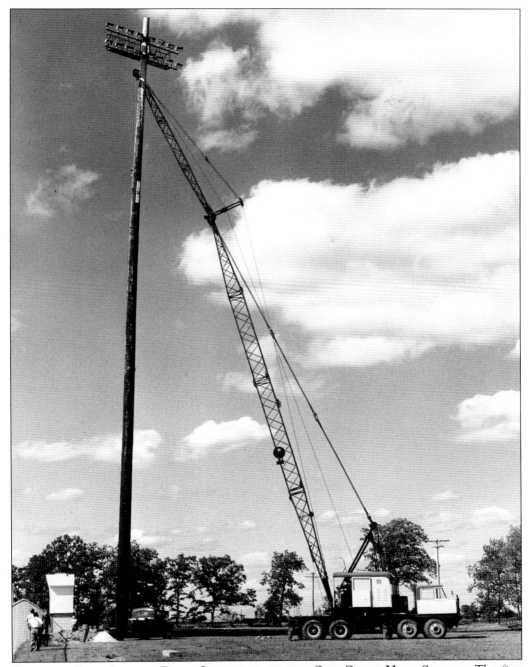

FOOTBALL FIELD LIGHTS, BEING INSTALLED AT THE OAK CREEK HIGH SCHOOL. The first night game held at the school was on September 11, 1964. The high school at this time had a student capacity of 1,500 and was constructed over two years at a cost of more than $3 million. (Courtesy of CNI Newspapers.)

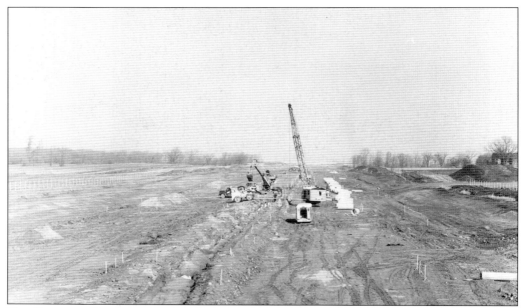

The Freeway Construction of Interstate 94 from Puetz Road, Looking North, in November 1964. (Courtesy of CNI Newspapers.)

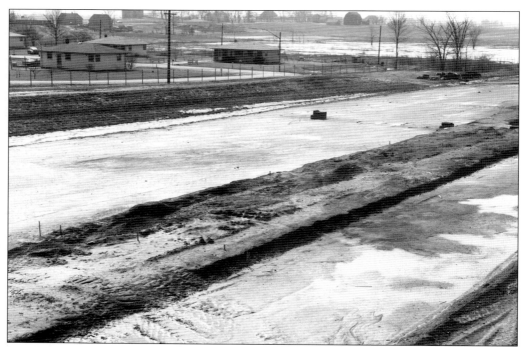

Interstate 94 Construction, Looking South on the Puetz Avenue Bridge. The Interstate 94 freeway was being built throughout the Oak Creek area. This part of the construction was done in the spring of 1965. (Courtesy of CNI Newspapers.)

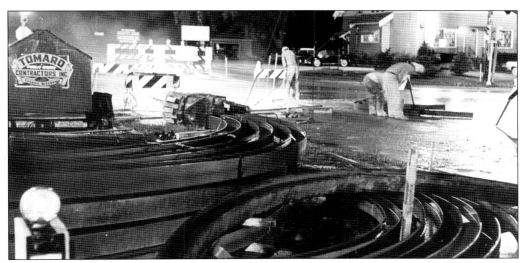

SEWER CONSTRUCTION ALONG THE ROUTE OF THE METROPOLITAN SEWERAGE DISTRICT. In this photo, the men are working on putting in a manhole on the corner of Howell and Puetz in September 1965. (Courtesy of CNI Newspapers.)

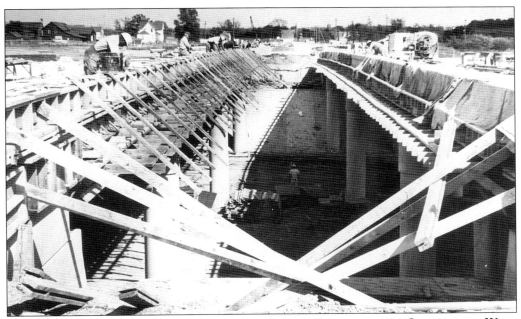

PREPARING FORMS FOR THE CONCRETE RAILING ON THE INTERSTATE 94 OVERPASS ON WEST RYAN ROAD, SEPTEMBER 1965. (Courtesy of CNI Newspapers.)

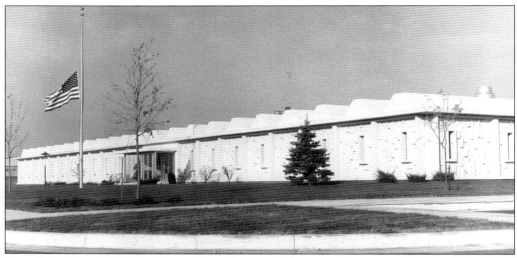

NEW CITY HALL, SHORTLY AFTER FINAL LANDSCAPING WAS COMPLETED. The building would accommodate the city's growing needs for a central location for the various city departments. (Courtesy of CNI Newspapers.)

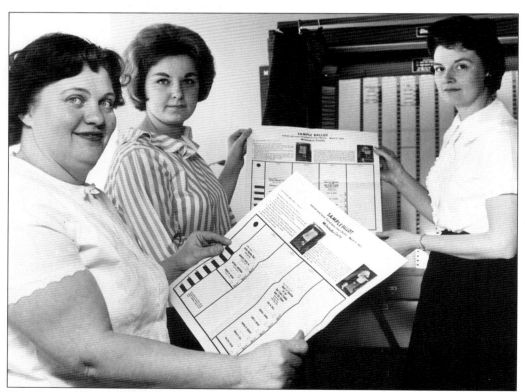

THE FIRST VOTING MACHINES FOR THE CITY OF OAK CREEK, MARCH 1965. Showing a sample of the voting ballots, from left to right are: City Clerk LaVerne Gutknecht, Secretary Sharon Lampe, and Deputy Clerk Mrs. Russell Willms. (Courtesy of CNI Newspapers.)

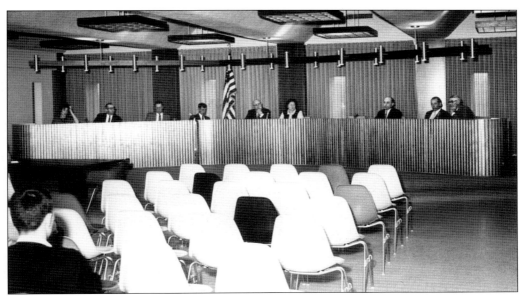

COMMON COUNCIL MEETING, MAY 1964. The meeting was held at what was at that time called the Civic Center, which is now the city hall. (Courtesy of CNI Newspapers.)

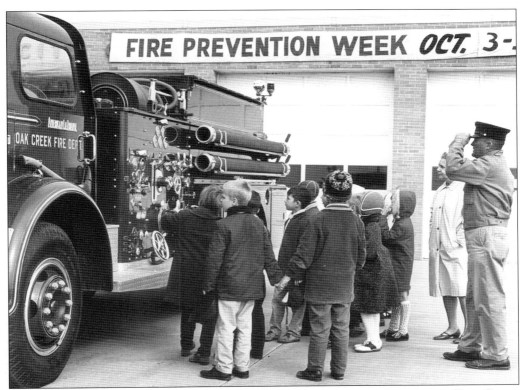

YOUNG SCHOOL VISITORS, GETTING AN UP-CLOSE INSPECTION OF ONE OF THE OAK CREEK FIRE DEPARTMENT'S FIRE TRUCKS. This was during Fire Prevention Week in October 1965. (Courtesy of CNI Newspapers.)

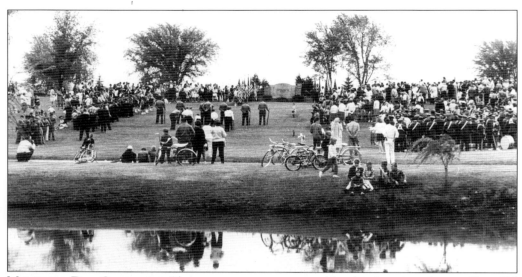

MEMORIAL DAY CEREMONY. The ceremony was sponsored by the American Legion Post 434 and was held at the Forest Hill Cemetery. The ceremony held at Forest Hill remains one of the biggest held in the Oak Creek area. (Courtesy of CNI Newspapers.)

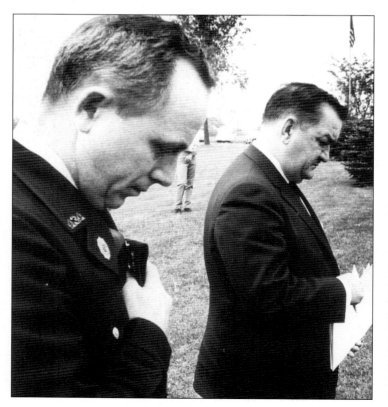

HONORED VETERANS. Honoring the Oak Creek veterans in the Memorial Day Ceremony were Donald Priest of Oak Creek's American Legion Post 434 and longtime Wisconsin Congressman Clement J. Zablocki. Zablocki was a featured speaker that day in 1965. (Courtesy of CNI Newspapers.)

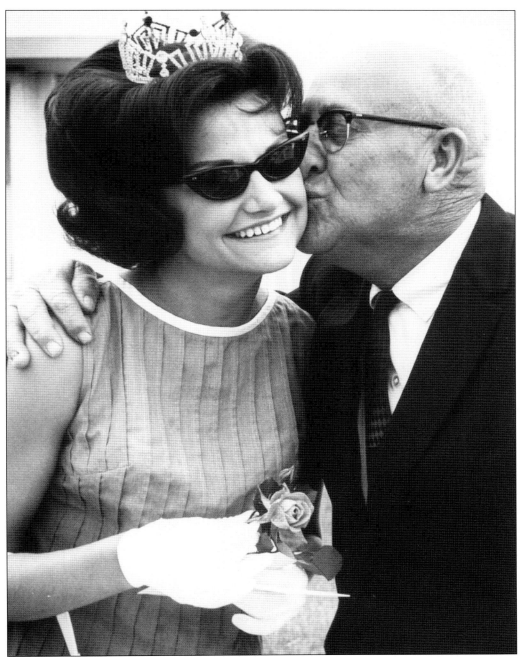

MISS OAK CREEK 1965, LINDA SCHUMACHER. Ms. Schumacher gets a good-luck kiss from Mayor Art Abendschein before she departs for the Miss Wisconsin pageant in Oshkosh. Abendschein was easily one of Oak Creek's most prominent citizens, being called the "George Washington of Oak Creek" by longtime friend and city attorney Anthony X. Basile. He would serve as the city's first mayor for over 16 years and was town chairman for six years prior to Oak Creek's incorporation. Abendschein Park on Drexel Avenue was named in his honor—a fitting tribute to one of the city's founders. (Courtesy of CNI Newspapers.)

ACKNOWLEDGMENTS

We would like to thank all those who provided the photographs and information for this book. Please note that photo credits were given to those that provided the photos to us, not necessarily the original owners. Although they are given credit after each picture, their efforts and generosity bears repeating: the Oak Creek Historical Society—especially archivist Carolyn Haack, LeRoy and Beulah Meyer, Eleanore and Alfred Hauerwas, Elroy and Nancy Honadel, LaVerne Gutknecht, Andrew Janiga, Gordon and Dolores Esch, CNI Newspapers—especially Dave Chvilicek, Karen Borchardt, Neal Raduenz, Duane Vanselow, Robert Morrow, and Violet Mahr. We would also like to mention the members of the Oak Creek Historical Society's Memorial Honor Roll who will not be able to see the final product, but contributed in their own way to make this book possible: Irene Ballbach, Melvin Kuhnke, Henry Mahr, Jack Hauter, Pete Gerber, Bob Rayeske, and Virginia Kling. All proceeds from the sale of this book go to the Oak Creek Historical Society.

This book is dedicated to the memory of our grandmothers, Florence Depner and Leonita Rowe, who taught us the importance of remembering the past.